G Bouturuc

4/6/2013

George Boutwell
George Boutwell's Texas Collection
3083 Highway 6
Clifton, Texas 76634

Manufactured in USA

ISBN 978-0-615-59657-0

Library of Congress Control Number: 2012903594

$45.00
ISBN 978-0-615-59657-0

54500>

9 780615 596570

PREFACE

For many years, when I have told my stories, I have constantly heard folks say, "you need to write a book" So after much procrastination and since no one stepped up and volunteered to write it for me, I decided that it was time to get in gear and get this book written. My approach in this book is different than any that I'm aware of, but I have always strived to be different without being weird.

I grew up poor and had to struggle for everything, so as a young boy, I often wished that I could just have a normal life. (as if there really is such a thing) As I've grown older, I have realized that my life experiences were quite unique and and that I am rich in life experience!

As far as I know, the stories in this book are accurate, but having a creative mind, I may have unintentionally embellished a few things. If anyone disagrees with any of the facts in this book, I can only say "write your own book"!

I have deliberately omitted the names of people that I felt might be hurt or embarrassed by my stories and have mentioned the names of the people that I have presented in a positive light.

Every other book about an Artist, (at least the ones I'm aware of) has listed the names of the people that bought the Painting below each Painting and usually include the rich and famous as if to state how connected the Artist is. I deliberately left out the names of my collectors because I can't remember a lot of them and I felt that it would be better to list none, than to list a few and hurt the feelings of the people that I can't remember! Some stories involve a painting being purchased, so I have included the names of those buyers in these stories.

There are lots of things that I left out, because I wanted to share the interesting and inspiring things and there were not enough pages to cram it all in anyway!

I owe much of my success to my wife Martha and my daughters Valerie and Kimberlee for their support. Knowing that they depended on me, often gave me the courage, to get back up and fight on when things seemed futile.

I thank Martha's Father, Gordon Stukes for his wisdom! Although he would not be considered successful by society's standards, he fathered eight children that would have been willing to die for him. He made his living doing what he enjoyed in spite of it not providing great financial rewards. When it seemed that the whole world was telling me that trying to be an Artist was stupid and impossible, Gordon Stukes told me "If you know what you want to do with your life and you don't try to achieve it, you will never be happy. It's better to try, even if you fail, than not to try at all."

I thank Jesus Christ for intervening in my life and guiding me in spite of my rejecting him earlier in my life.

As a kid, I was a dreamer and was often criticized for thinking I could do the impossible. Hopefully, my story will inspire at least one other dreamer to reach for their dreams.

-George Boutwell

TABLE OF CONTENTS

BEEN DOWN THAT ROAD is the most frequent thing I hear when folks are looking at this Painting. I had just photographed the old dance hall at Garfield, Texas and decided to take a shortcut back to the main road and found this delightful tree lined lane.

THE BEGINNING
(obviously)

I was born in 1943 during World War II in East Hartford, Connecticut (I couldn't help it), I should have been born in Texas, so I guess you would have to call it some kind of birth defect. My Father's dream was to become a preacher, a dream he would have to wait to realize until he was in his sixties. As a result of my Father's religious beliefs, he refused to fight in World War II and we were sent to

George and Sadie Osgood Boutwell and little Georgie before the tragedy

a government work camp for conscientious objectors in Michigan.

My Mother died in the camp due to complications from a miscarriage and lack of medical attention. I was sent to live with my Grandmother in Connecticut for the duration of the war. After the war, my father was released from the work camp and came to Connecticut and stayed with us while he was adjusting to being free.

Prior to my Mother's death, my Father and Mother had become interested in a new type of medicine that was beginning to take hold, known at the time as Natural Hygienist Medicine which involved fasting and a vegetarian diet.

My Father had eight brothers of whom, five, who were old enough, had gone to war and one had been killed in action. My Father's brother Elwin had been crippled as a teenager and was not able to serve in the military and was the only one of my Fathers brothers who wasn't angry at my Father for refusal to serve in the military.

My Father and Elwin bought an old school bus, loaded some beds and an ice chest into it, took me and we hit the road. The details of how we ended up in Indiana are not real clear but my Father and Elwin became employed by a Natural Hygienist Clinic in Ligoneer, Indiana which was in an old Mansion known as Melrose Manor. The Doctor there was a woman from India that they called Dr. Rider (I'm not sure if Rider was the correct spelling of her name but that's how it sounded). It wasn't long before the authorities shut Melrose Manor down and Uncle Elwin went back to Connecticut in the school bus and my Father and I hitchhiked to Tennessee where he worked in another Natural Hygienist clinic for a couple of months.

My Father was offered a job with Dr. Shelton in San Antonio, Texas. Dr. Shelton had written most of the books on Natural Hygienist Medicine and my Father was determined to get to San Antonio, so we stuck out our thumbs and took off hitchhiking to San Antonio. ⬥

CRO... I C THE TEXAS LINE:

Bear in mind, that lot's of folks hitchhiked in the 1940's, but with a four year old by his side, my Father got rides easier than most folks and that made me feel important. Well, there we were in Arkansas, and it was a hot summer day and some how my hitchhiking skills were way off that day, because we weren't getting a ride. Off in the distance, down the road, we saw something large moving very slowly toward us and as it got closer, we could see that it was a wagon loaded with cotton, being pulled by two mules and there, up on the seat, sat a kindly looking old Negro with a large white beard, a wide straw hat and bib overalls (I was awestruck because, I was sure he was Uncle Remus and I couldn't wait to find out how Br'er Rabbit was doing!)

As he pulled up beside us, he looked down and said "Ya'll jess well get on". My Father put me up on the seat and climbed on after me and we headed off for the cotton gin which was just over the Texas state line! I crawled up on the load of cotton, where I could see over their heads and had a good time waving to cars that passed by. Uncle Remus let us off at the cotton gin and my feet landed on Texas soil!

A LITTLE EXCITEMENT

We walked away from the cotton gin for what seemed to be miles and miles, when, what I think was a 1938 Buick sedan stopped a ways ahead of us and a man got out and ran into the woods. Then the car backed up to where we were walking and the driver told us to get in, if we needed a ride. We got into the Buick with the driver and his wife and the car pulled away leaving the man in the woods. My father said, "what about the man who ran into the woods?" and the driver said, "we picked him up, hitchhiking over in Arkansas and he pulled a pistol and robbed us, then told us where to stop and made his getaway. We didn't figure a man with a little boy would do us any harm so we picked you up! We rode a ways down the road and the driver asked my Father where we were headed. My Father told

him that he had a job waiting in San Antonio and the driver said "we are headed to San Antonio to visit some of our Kin Folk!" A little while later, the driver asked my Father if he had any money and my father replied, "about 20 bucks" The driver said, if you will buy lunch and some gas, we'll take you to San Antonio and I'm sure our relatives will pay you back when we get there!

LIVING IN SAN ANTONIO

Dr. Shelton's clinic was a large complex which was somewhere near the Airport because I would sit for hours on the big front porch watching the Airplanes land and take off. The standard treatment of patients was simple. The patient would be put on a fast with nothing to eat and only distilled water to drink for several days, with mostly sunbathing and bed rest. The fast would then be changed to fruit juice and more sunbathing and finally thepatient would be given fruits, vegetables and nuts to eat for several more days. The treatment usually lasted about 3 months and it seemed that everyone got cured.

I played in an area next to the clinic that had once been some kind of building but all that was left was an open air basement with rock steps that went down to the bottom and I told everyone that it was "Deep in the Heart of Texas!".

I started school in a one room school with all 8 grades, each in its own row starting with first grade on the right and progressing to the eighth grade on the left. The school was near enough to the clinic that I could walk to school and I had to walk over an old iron bridge that crossed what I was sure was a raging river.

A couple of the eighth grade boys took great delight in grabbing me by the arms and dangling me over the edge of the bridge and listening to me scream as they threatened to drop me into the river. I told my Father and Dr. Shelton about what the eighth grade boys had done and we piled into Dr. Shelton's Cadillac convertible and drove to the school. I don't know what the teacher did to the boys but they never bothered me again!

The bridge in this Painting is pretty close to the one I remember, that the eighth graders dangled me over when I was in the first grade in San Antonio! The following tells the reasons for the Painting that I did in 1977.

I'VE CROSSED THAT BRIDGE BEFORE

While driving on the IH35 access road south of Hewitt, Texas , I had a choice to make, either to get back on IH35, or take a dirt road of unknown destination. Many of the people who have seen this Painting have said, "I've Crossed That Bridge Before!"

Due to my not having much contact with other kids, I hadn't learned much in the way of social skills and had trouble expressing myself verbally. I would get frustrated and draw pictures of what I was trying to communicate and this got me praise and the other kids called me an Artist. I liked the sound of "Artist" so I kept on drawing pictures to the point that I probably drove them crazy. ✣

CALIFORNIA HERE WE COME

My Father met and fell in love with a woman named Betty in San Antonio and they decided to marry. The details of how and why they decided to move to California are unclear, but my Father had a job offer to work as the Doctor in a Natural Hygienist Clinic in Altadena, California. My Father and I hitchhiked to California to get established and Betty joined us later.

The one adventure that stands out in my mind about the California trip was outside of Needles, California.

We were out in the desert, trying to get a ride and it was close to sundown. We saw a pack of Coyotes cross the road in single file about 100 yards in front of us. A while later the Coyotes crossed the road in front of us but a little closer to us this time. In a little while we saw the Coyotes cross the road behind us even closer than before. We realized that the Coyotes were circling us, getting ever closer and closer and we were getting very nervous about what their intent might be. As the last rays of sunshine were fading and the Coyotes were close enough that we could make eye contact with them, a car pulled up and the door swung open and we ran like a couple of Rabbits and jumped into the car!

We got to the Clinic in Altadena which was up in the mountains and as I remember, there was a spectacular view of the valley below. I was enrolled in a school down in the valley, (still in the First Grade) and rode a bus to school. Shortly after getting settled in Altadena, the clinic was shut down by the

authorities and my Father and I moved into a house in Los Angeles and Betty joined us there. I was enrolled in another school (still in the First Grade) for a short time and then we moved to Pasadena and I finished the First Grade in my fourth school!

My Father took a job working for a man (whose last name, I think was Doolen) who had invented a snack that he hoped would compete with the potato chip. The snack just wasn't catching on and when Mr. Doolen couldn't make payroll, he offered his employees stock in the company, instead on money. My Father said we couldn't eat stock so he quit the job with that company that is known today as Frito Lay! The employees that stayed with Mr. Doolen all retired very rich!

It turned out that Betty was a Schizophrenic and could be a very sweet lady at one moment and become extremely violent in the next moment. She went on a screaming rant because of some large cockroaches, tore up the house and beat me severely (I guess I must have resembled a Cockroach). My Father decided to send me back to live with my Grandmother in Connecticut. ⬩

BACK TO CONNECTICUT

My Father answered an add in the paper that said that a man named Harry would be driving to Massachusetts and was looking for passengers to share the expenses of the trip. Harry drove a Hudson, the kind that looked like a big bathtub, and along with two elderly women, Harry and I headed for the east coast. I had a toy airplane with a propeller that turned and amused myself by holding it out the car window, in the wind, to make the propeller spin. I remember stopping at the Grand Canyon and not much else about the trip. Harry let the two elderly women off in Pennsylvania and got me to my Grandmother's house around suppertime and my Grandmother insisted that he stay for supper. In retrospect, I don't really understand why my Father

sent me off across the country with a total stranger but fortunately for me, Harry turned out to be a great guy and I couldn't have been in better hands.

My Grandfather worked as a machinist at the Pratt and Whitney Aircraft factory which was East Hartford's largest employer and they lived in a low income housing project named Mayberry Village. I stayed with my Grandparents in a three bedroom apartment along with my two cousins Dorothy and Eddie, whose Mother had died of polio and

my Uncle Jim and Uncle Haven (Dorothy and Eddie's Father). I lived with my Grandmother and Grandfather until the middle of the fourth grade, at which time my Father sent for me because he was convinced that Betty was doing better (My Father and Betty had moved to Texas while I had been at my Grandmother's).

Shortly before departing for Texas, I experienced what I consider to be one of my biggest moments as an Artist. I attended Woodlawn Elementary school, which had eight

The Yellow Car below is a Hudson like the one Harry drove in the story above! The Ponca Motel is in Abilene, Texas.

grades. Each year a contest was held to produce a Christmas mural that was put on the bulletin board in front of the Principal's office. Each student that participated in the contest, produced a small scale version of their proposed mural. The Principal and the school's only art teacher were the judges. To my surprise, I won the contest, beating out all of the older kids and I got to enlarge my artwork to four feet by eight feet and at this point, I was sure that I would become an artist when I grew up. 🪶

FLYBOY DELUXE

My Uncle Haven, (the only one with a car) put me on an airplane at the Hartford airport and I flew to New York, changed planes, flew to Chicago, changed planes, flew to Dallas, changed planes and flew to Austin. Each time I boarded a plane, I was greeted by the pilot who gave me a pin with a set of wings. The pilot of the Dallas to Austin flight let me sit in the co-pilot's seat when the co-pilot took a break. I arrived in Austin with four sets of wings, totally convinced that with my experience I could fly the plane if only they would let me.

I soon learned that Betty was not better and my life was becoming a living hell, because I had to spend three hours alone with her each day after school, before my Father came home from work. She was totally unpredictable, switching from being kind and loving to violent and uncontrollable because of the least little thing. She loved the arts and classical music; and when she was listening to one of her symphonies, something as simple as a creaking floorboard would set her off into a violent rage. I was attacked and beaten several times and she even chased me with a butcher knife, plunging it thru the bathroom door that I had been fortunate enough to lock before she got to me. I escaped through the bathroom window, climbed a tree and stayed up there until my Father got home from work. One day I realized something that undoubtedly saved my life. Betty considered Art to be very cultural and I noticed that she treated me very lovingly when I was drawing or painting. I developed a strategy for survival: each day after school, I would tiptoe into my room and get my paints out and I would be safe! My new strategy worked like a charm and we got along famously after that! To this date, every time the world starts kicking me around, I can get out the paints and I feel safe!

My poor Father would come home and invariably make some blunder and Betty would vent all of her wrath on him. At the end of the fourth grade, I was put back on an airplane to Connecticut to stay with my Grandmother again. My Father soon moved to Connecticut and stayed with all the rest of us in that apartment. About a year later, Betty arrived in Connecticut and my Father moved in with her, leaving me at my Grandmothers, but things didn't go well and Betty went back to Texas in less than a year.

Meanwhile, I became a small scale entrepreneur, gathering and selling soda bottles, making and selling Christmas wreaths, selling Christmas cards door to door in the projects where we lived and in the adjoining neighborhoods where the "Rich Folks" lived. By the eighth grade, I had a pretty good little stash of cash and my Father borrowed it from me and bought us bus tickets to Texas, because, he said "Betty was better". When we got back to Texas, we lived out in the country near Manchaca, south of Austin, and Betty wasn't better but I knew how to control her and she was my Father's problem this time! In about a month my Father rented a one room apartment in Austin near the University of Texas and he and I moved in, leaving Betty in the country. The move made it three different schools for me to finish the eighth grade. Not long after our move into Austin, a Methodist preacher stopped to see Betty and during the visit she went into one of her schizophrenic episodes and the preacher had her committed to the State Mental Hospital where she spent the rest of her life! ⬤

The first place that my Father and I lived in was a garage apartment that was behind an old house and directly across the alley from a fraternity house. Our landlady, who lived in the house in front, was in her nineties and crazy as a loon. The thing I remember most about her was that she would patrol the picket fence between her yard and the parking lot for the fraternity house and Hirsch's Drug Store and upon finding a car parked too close to her fence, she would beat the car with a broom causing minor damage. (had she been younger and stronger there might have been wrecked cars all along the fence.) The garage apartment rocked back and forth when the wind blew and the fraternity boys were loud at all hours of the night. When the rent came due, my Father and I moved to a one room apartment about a block away on 28th street. Our new residence was upstairs in an old house that had four one room apartments upstairs. We shared a bathroom with the other apartments, and our landlady lived downstairs. My Father worked for Austin Linen Service where he drove a truck and delivered fresh linen to restaurants and the linen truck was our only transportation. ⬤

I attended University Junior High School on the other side of the University of Texas and since the students from Alan Junior High (which had burned) attended the school in the afternoon we got to school at 6:00 am and finished at noon. My Father and I would pile into the linen truck and he would drop me off at school on his way to work and I would walk home after school. On my walk home I realized that Waller Creek flowed along San Jacinto Blvd. and wound up at Hemphill Park a couple of blocks from our apartment. I started walking the creek bottom out of curiosity and soon discovered that the University students were throwing soda bottles in the creek. I got me a toe sack (sometimes called a burlap bag outside of Texas) and picked up the soda bottles every day on my way home and sold them at the convenience store near our apartment for two cents each and was on my way to becoming a salvage tycoon! After I got home, I worked at Big Bear Grocery Store as a sack boy for 25 cents an hour for a month and then went to work at Hirsch Drug Store in their soda fountain for 25 cents an hour plus tips! I saved almost all of the money I earned and hid it in my closet and by the time I turned sixteen I had saved $165.

By this time, I was attending Austin High School and riding the city bus to school. After school, I would walk down to the 5th and 6th street area which was lined with used car lots. I found a 1948 Chevrolet on the Jim Bell Motors lot and tried to buy it, but, being a minor, I was told that my Father needed to sign the papers. I told my Father that I wanted to buy a car and he agreed to sign for it, if I could pay for it. My Father thought we were playing a game, so we drove to the car lot in the linen truck and went into Mr Bell's office and sat down to do some dealing. Mr. Bell said "son, how do you plan to pay for this car?" I pulled the $165 out of my pocket and laid it on his desk. I don't remember who was the most shocked, my Father or Mr. Bell, but now they knew that this was not a game. My Father said, "where did you get all of that money (more than he made in a month) and why didn't you tell me about it?" and I said "the last time you knew I had any money, you borrowed it to pay our bus fare to Texas and I never saw it again!"

The portrait of the Big Texan on the building is a portrait from memory of Mr. Bell, the man who sold me my first used car in 1959 and actually the building is also a portrait from memory. I added cars from the era and had I realized that I would be writing this story, I might have included a 1948 Chevrolet!

Let's regress back to Junior High for a couple of more stories. A block from our apartment was a drive-inn restaurant called Martin's Kumbak (affectionately known to this day as "Dirty's") Dirty's has a second story with an outside stairway and a boy named Roy Schafer and his Mother, Mary lived in that second story apartment. Roy and I became best friends and spent much of our time together for the next four years.

DIRTY'S is in the 2800 block of Guadalupe, an Austin legend since 1926. (Texas" oldest Drive In Restaurant) Actually named Martin's Kumbak Place, It's been called Dirty's by the locals for generations. "Dirty's" is rather sentimental to me because, when I was a teenager, I lived about a block away and my best friend Roy Schafer lived in the apartment above the restaurant. Many Saturday and Sunday mornings we would clean the parking lot and would be paid with a Cheeseburger and a Malt!

Roy's Father "Andy" was a carhop at Dirty's and lived in an apartment in an old house across the street. (Roy's parents were divorced). Mary became like a second Mother to me and taught me to love Jalapeno Peppers and Mexican Food. Mary was 100 percent Mexican and fiercely proud of her heritage. Roy's Father, although having a German last name, was also of Mexican descent. In the late 50's, Mexicans were considered inferior by most white folks but Roy was able to gain acceptance because of his German last name and outgoing personality.

Mary, however refused to accept being Mexican as something inferior and to this day, every time I think of using the terms Hispanic, Latino or Spanish, I can hear Mary's voice insisting that everyone refer to her as Mexican!

Roy and I joined the Boy Scouts and had many adventures at Camp Tom Wooten and at our Scoutmaster, Joe Neal's Ranch. Joe Neal's son John was also in Scouts and we spent lots of time with John and his parents.

My Father, bless his soul, had raised me to believe that "Rich Folks" were wicked and that it was "easier for a camel to go thru the eye of a needle than for a rich man to enter Heaven." Now I'm not sure if Joe and Clairese Neal were rich but, by comparison to Roy and I, they were. Joe was a professor at the University of Texas and owned a big house on the west side, a new Pontiac and two ranches. These were the first "Rich Folks" that I had any close contact with and I found them to be absolutely wonderful people especially, John's Mother, Clairese who was possibly the kindest person I've ever known.

WHEELIN AND DEALIN

In the 3 years before graduation from High School, I would own 10 more cars for a total of 11 in High School. Now, don't get the idea that I was a shrewd trader and left High School in a Rolls Royce, the truth couldn't be more opposite. The 48 Chevrolet blew an engine and I won a 1950 DeSoto (another story I'll get

to later!) The DeSoto blew an engine and I sold it and the 48 Chevrolet as junk for $100. I bought a 1948 Ford with the savings I'd made working at Hirsch Drug Store and some other income that I was making on the side (I'll get to the sideline income later). The 48 Ford got traded in on a 55 Ford which I was able to buy, making monthly payments. The 55 Ford got repossessed and this began my relationship with Jack Mason Motors. Jack had a combination car lot and junk yard out on South First Street and operated what he called a note lot. Jack kept a ledger and I would give him $20 down and drive the car (which was still in his name so my Father didn't need to sign)

I'd stop by after work once a month and give him another $20. Jack took a lot of trade-in cars from the new car dealerships that were so far gone that the dealers didn't want to mess with them. Jack had a good mechanic who would get the cars running, good enough to sell. My first car from Jack was a 41 Chevrolet and when it cratered, I called Jack, he sent his wrecker out and picked up me and the car, brought me back to the lot where Jack told me to pick out another car. He told me the amount he would reduce my debt, added the car I had selected to the note and I drove off in a 1948 Oldsmobile! This process would be repeated several more times and I subsequently drove a 1948 English Ford, a 1938 Buick, a 1936 Ford, a 1936 Pontiac and finally a 1950 Chevrolet which I ultimately paid off! ✛

MEMORABLE PRANKS

While I was walking Waller Creek in Junior High School, collecting soda bottles, I noticed a little structure in the creek that appeared to be some kind of scientific survey that measured water levels. I also noticed that up stream, about 100 feet, the creek split into two creeks and that the east fork went into a tunnel under San Jacinto Boulevard. A devilish idea blasted into my mind, that was just too good not to act on. There was a boy named Kenny who occasionally walked the creek with me and I shared my fiendish idea with him and he joined me in my plot. We went into the tunnel about half way under San Jacinto Boulevard and built a dam with rocks and mud. The dam was about thirty inches high and invisible from the street. After a long stretch without rain, we went into the tunnel and broke the dam, causing a small wall of water to rush down the creek, which we were sure would totally baffle those scientists who were studying the data from the survey station!

While at summer Boy Scout camp at Camp Tom Wooten, Roy killed a large rattlesnake that was near the shooting range (Roy was an incredibly good shot!) We cut off the rattles and attached them to a spring that we had found and stationed ourselves behind the latrine in the dark. The latrine had an open back for clean out and when another Scout would get situated on the seat and get into deep concentration, we would flip the spring with the snake rattle on it and the boy would come blasting out of the latrine, pulling up his pants while at a dead run!

One of our Scoutmaster, Joe Neal's ranches was on the San Antonio River near the small town of Charco. There were several new scouts who were on the camping trip to this ranch and Roy and I and Eric Schmidt were in charge of conducting a snipe hunt which was a tradition for initiating new Scouts.

Traditionally, the young Scouts were placed about 20 foot apart out in the dark, with a toe sack, a flashlight and two sticks. The boys were told to put the flashlight in the back of the sack, straddle the sack and hold one edge open with their teeth, while clicking the sticks together. The clicking sticks were supposed to attract the attention of the Snipes and they would see the light in the sack and run into the sack and the boy would quickly close the sack capturing the Snipe

Eric had noticed a herd of sheep in

15

the next pasture and got Roy and I to become his a accomplices in crime. We opened the gate and stampeded the sheep onto the Snipe Hunters. Luckily no one got hurt and no one caught a Snipe or a sheep but Roy, Eric and I caught Hell from Joe Neal, who made us herd the sheep back into their pasture (easier said than done!) and then we were sent home early. ✛

When I had the 48 Ford, I was the only kid in our little gang that had a car and all of my deadbeat buddies wanted to ride around all night but never seemed to have any money to help with the gas. I got tired of this and went to the local auto parts store and bought two toggle switches. I mounted both switches beside the steering column out of sight of the passengers in the car. The left switch was wired to the gas gauge and the right one was wired to the ignition. I would drive a while and flip the left switch and the gas gauge would go to empty and I would tell my friends that "this thing's running on fumes."

I would drive until I saw a gas station down the street and when we were about half a block from the station, I would flip the right switch and the engine would die. We would all jump out and push the car to the gas station, where I would say I was broke and my passengers would start digging for change, collectively coming up with around a dollar which at the time would buy close to 5 gallons of gas! ✛

FOOTBALL STAR AND MARTIAL ARTS EXPERT

We lived in a poor white neighborhood that was adjacent to the Black neighborhood from 12th street to 19th Street and the Mexican neighborhood from 12th street south. As a result, all three groups intermingled. We all had poverty in common and for the most part got along pretty well.

One of the highlights of the weekends, that were not home games for the University of Texas, was a "sand lot", "no pads or helmets" football game, at Memorial Stadium. We would choose sides and play hard core tackle football. This may not be politically correct, but "political correctness" hadn't been invented in the 1950's. The schools at the time, were still segregated and the Blacks had their own separate schools, otherwise these Black boys that we were playing football with would have undoubtedly been the varsity stars at Austin High. Those Black boys were natural born great football players and made us Whites and Mexicans look like girls by comparison, but they still allowed us to play football with them.

Our game got the attention of some West Austin boys including a few Austin High varsity players and we challenged them to a game. The game turned out to be a "rout" with a score of somewhere around 90 to 6 in favor of the east side boys! The west side fullback was a huge guy, I'll call Bull Dog, who ended up with a college athletic scholarship but he was out of his league when it came to playing against those Black boys. After a couple of plays Bull Dog complained about the roughness of our side and our full back, an equally large Black boy named Ovan told him, "This is a man's game, if it's too rough for you, go home to yo Momma"

Several plays later, Bull Dog came charging thru the line and I flung my 115 pound body in front of him and he tripped over me and went down. He came up red in the face and shouted at me to stay out of his way or he would make a "Grease Spot" out of me. A few plays later Bull Dog came charging thru the line again and I (totally by accident) caught him in the Adam's Apple with my elbow and he hit the ground gasping for breath and turning blue. When he was finally able to catch his breath, he got up with fire in his eyes and told me he was going to beat hell out of me.

So here I was, a 115 pound shrimp, facing a 275 pound raging bull and I knew I had no chance unless I could perform a miracle of some kind.

Alas, my creative mind came thru with a spectacular idea that may have saved my life! I backed up and took my foot and scraped a line in the dirt in front of him and went into a Karate stance with my hands up as if to use them like axes and said "what I just did to you is nothing, step over that line and I'll show you what else I can do to you." My heart was racing like a sewing machine when Ovan said loudly to a couple of the other Black boys "Have ya'll ever seen George do the Karate? Man, he gonna kill that boy, he's bad with that Karate." Thanks to Ovan's quick thinking, Bull Dog stood there thinking, then backed up and said "aw hell, lets play football" I thanked Ovan for backing me up and he laughed and said "we wasn't gonna let him whup you too bad". ⬟

THE BIG WINNER
(sort of)

Roy and his Mother had moved to an apartment on 12th street, which was a closer walk to her work. The apartment was behind a car dealership named Big Volume Simmons and they had a used car lot across Lamar Boulevard from the new car dealership. Simmons was having a big promotion called the "Cotton Pickin, Cotton Patch Sale" and were giving away a bale of cotton at the dealership and a $300 used car at the used car lot. The used car lot was run by a man we called Bubba who was hostile to kids. "Beat it, punks, you ain't got no money" would be Bubba's reply when Roy and I would step onto the lot to look at the used cars. Since my 48 Chevy was broke down, I decided I would win the $300 used car. Each day, when Bubba went to lunch, I would sneak over and grab a bunch of entry blanks, go back to Roy's, fill them out and go back the next day when Bubba went to lunch, put the entry blanks in the hopper and grab more entry blanks, repeating the process for several days. Lo and behold, I got a letter (we didn't have a telephone) stating that I was the winner of the $300 used car! I was afraid Bubba would go nuts if I showed up alone and since my Father had the same name as mine I asked him to help me claim the prize. We drove to the car lot in the linen truck and my Father presented the letter. Bubba was sharper than I thought and the instant that he saw me, he was on to my little deception (steam seemed to be coming out of his ears!) Not wanting to have a conflict with my Father, Bubba gave my Father some papers, took us to the back of the lot and handed my Father the keys to a beat up 1950 DeSoto. My father said "is this thing really worth $300?" Bubba said "as far as I'm concerned, it is". The DeSoto belched enough

smoke to double as a mosquito fogger and I drove it for about three weeks before it threw a rod. I got $50 for it at the junk yard so I guess you could say I won $50 and Bubba is probably still laughing!

A DARK PERIOD IN MY LIFE

During the time that I had the 48 Ford, my Father had met a woman and had fallen in love and I was on my own, due to him never being

around to supervise and I began to run wild. I had left Scouting when I got a car and became interested in girls. I had lost contact with John Neal's family and began to run with some new friends. Due to my Mother's death and my Stepmother's violence and other heart breaks, I was very vulnerable, craved acceptance and was willing to go along with the gang. I had no real values or morals during this time in my life and considered myself to be an atheist. I was very good at lying

This Painting is a depiction of the Used Car Lot that I refer to in the story above and the caption below is what I wrote for the description in my catalog, so if you read the story, you know that there was more to the story!
BIG VOLUME BUBBA When I was a teenager in Austin, a friend of mine lived behind a car lot named Big Volume Simmons and they sold both new and used cars on both sides of Lamar Boulevard. Bubba was a salesman for Simmons, but he acted like he owned the place so I made his dream come true in this painting!

and felt absolutely no remorse. My new friends were exciting to run with and I began to steal like they did. Our goal was to run around and cruise town and not have to work or worry about having enough money to do our running. We would steal anything we thought we could use or sell, but none of our thieving activities generated very much money and most of what we did involved lots of risk. We siphoned gas, which in addition to being risky, didn't taste good at all. We burglarized homes and businesses, when we were sure no one was around.

One night, when we were trying to think of what we would steal next, I remembered my days of collecting soda bottles and stopped at the back of a dormitory, where I knew there were vending machines and we stole all of the empty bottles and took them to a convenience store and cashed them in. We had stolen empty bottles for a few nights when I got the bright idea to break open the vending machines that contained the soda and get the money and all

the cold soda we could carry. We found that vending machines were an easy target and that with a crowbar we could easily get lots of money, drinks, candy and cigarettes. It was quick and we got cash to run on and didn't have to try to sell anything; we could quickly do our little dirty deed and have the rest of the night for running around. (this is the sideline money I referred to earlier).

I used lots of my ill gotten money to buy speed equipment to "soup up" the 48 Ford which I envisioned being necessary to run from the police. My Father's resentment of rich people made it easy for me to rationalize my anti social behavior. Roy was aware of my new lifestyle and although he refused to get involved in any of my crime activities, he remained my friend.

My crime spree came to an abrupt end one day at an Austin High football game. I was standing up, cheering, when I suddenly felt a jabbing pain in my back. I turned and made eye contact with a man

whose reputation on the street was that of a "Hit Man." He was holding a large knife with about 3/16" of the point sticking out from his fingers and had rammed the point of the knife into my back. He was known as the "Slasher" and I won't tell you anything about him because he might still be living! I was shaking like a leaf and he pulled close to me and said that his friends owned the vending machines that we had been burglarizing. He said, "you are just a kid, so I'll give you another chance but if you value your life, you'll never break into another vending machine! Tell your buddies, the same goes for them!"His composure changed rather abruptly and his eyes seemed to soften and he said,"you seem like a good kid, get out of this stuff while you still can, don't make the same mistakes I did!" He turned and vanished into the crowd. What fools we had been, it never dawned on us that vending machines were an all cash business and an ideal way for organized criminals to launder money!
(We had been robbing the Mob!)

I'll remember his eyes as long as I live and I guess he saw in me, a little of himself when he was younger. He probably knew too much at this point, to leave his life of evil and stay alive and I actually felt sorry for him. You might wonder how a Hit Man, that was rumored to have killed two of the worst and meanest thugs in Austin kept from being arrested and I suspect that the police were aware of his activities and were thankful that he had done them a big favor! I told my buddies what the Slasher had said and they decided to lay off of the vending machines and focus on other crimes.

I was tired of looking over my shoulder and worrying all the time like some kind of frightened animal, so I refused to run with them anymore and as a result was badly beaten up a couple of times. A couple of the group ended up in prison (one of them for murder), two of them were murdered and the guy that beat me up so badly, died in a homeless shelter.

Other than myself, only two others that I know of have straightened out and seem to have become good productive citizens!.

It seemed like I was never punished for my crimes, but many years later when I had opened my own Art gallery and picture frame shop, bought a motor home and a two story victorian home and was enjoying more success than I ever thought I would, we were the victims of three burglaries in just two weeks. Thieves broke into our gallery and stole all of our air compressors and nail guns and several paintings, my motor home was broken into and my camera equipment was stolen, and a hand carved antique mantle was stolen from our home.

I was furious, I felt so violated and the police were totally indifferent about all of this. My anger and grief built up and I was getting very depressed. I headed out for an Art show in Lubbock and as I was driving, I suddenly realized that I had just paid an old debt. I had felt the pain and grief that I had caused others and I realized that my

pay back had waited until I had something to lose. I felt like a great weight had been lifted off of my shoulders!

Almost two months had passed with no contact from the police, when I got a call telling me that they had recovered three of my stolen paintings. When I was recovering my paintings I was told that the police had broken up a burglary and drug ring. The couple that were arrested, lived in a fashionable house in the rich part of town and drove expensive cars and were partners with a couple in San Antonio. They were drug dealers and would trade drugs for items that were stolen and would take the goods to San Antonio where the other couple would sell the goods thru pawn shops and in turn the San Antonio couple would give their stolen goods to the Austin couple who would sell the stolen San Antonio goods thru the Austin pawn shops. This exchange kept any of the stolen merchandise from being tracked. The reason that the police were able to recover my three paintings, was because my paintings were hanging on the walls of the Austin couple's house. Apparently the Austin couple had visited my gallery, selected their favorite paintings and sent their drug addict burglars to our gallery to retrieve them. It amazes me that, indirectly, the pay back for my dishonesty resulted in the elimination of a lot of potential losses for many other people! ✛

MOVING ON UP!

My Father announced one day, that I was going to have a new Stepmother and I met his new love and her Son, Rodney King, my soon to be Step Brother for the first time. We soon moved to Kinney Avenue in South Austin (a pretty good neighborhood) to a real house and with the combined income of both of their jobs, our lifestyle improved substantially! My Father quit the linen company, bought a station wagon, began wearing a suit and selling insurance. We even had a telephone and a television! My new Stepmother was very status

conscious and insisted that I dress better and took me down to Jack Morton's Men's Store on Congress Avenue and bought me a bunch of new clothes. She insisted that I wasn't going to attract any debutantes in my old 48 ford, so she and my Father got me to trade in the 48 Ford on a 55 Ford (complete with monthly payments) which at the time was only five years old.

I now looked more like one of those rich kids! Rodney was five years younger than I was and wasn't very thrilled with having an older Brother since he had been the center of his Mother's attention for so long. I on the other hand was delighted at the prospect of living in a better place with more luxuries such as not having to share a bathroom with the neighbors! ✛

SUPER DUPER SERVICE!

School was out for the summer and I went looking for a summer job. There was and old Mobil station at 31st and Guadalupe that had been closed down for a long time and as I

was passing by, I noticed a car in the drive way and a man inside the station. I went in and asked the man if the station was re-opening and if so, did they need any summer help. The man's name was Henry Sasse (the Mobil distributor for the Austin area) and he was either a good judge of character or very reckless, because he told me "I won't pay you a salary but if you want to run this station on a commission basis, you can take over today." He said, "you will get five cents for every gallon of gas you sell, ten cents for each quart of motor oil and all of the service money for lube jobs and tire repairs", I said, "I'll do it!"

The first week was slow and a few boys from the neighborhood started hanging around and I had a brainstorm, inspired by Mark Twain's Tom Sawyer. Getting to hang out in a gas station was something most boys in the 1950's dreamed of, so I told them that if they wanted to work on their cars, use the grease rack or wash their cars that they were welcome, under one condition.

That was, that when a car drove up to the pumps, every boy agreed to drop what they were doing and help me give the new customer service like they had never seen! So every car got their tires checked, windshields washed, carpets vacuumed, oil, water and battery water checked while getting their gas tank filled.

The boys had fun and we built a customer base in a big hurry! The station had three service bays and a retired mechanic named R. L. Gardner offered to rent one of the bays to work on the cars of a few customers that he had continued to service. By the end of the month I was making more money than my Father and begged him to let me quit school and get rich. My Father refused to let me quit school and in September my entrepreneurial venture came to an end. The station got turned over to a college student who promptly ran my friends off and got rid of Mr. Gardner because he cursed too much. The station went from super service to barely any service and was out of business within two months.

My Father and Stepmother insisted that they would make the payments on the 55 Ford so I could concentrate on my school work and be on the track team. I woke up one February morning to the sound of a wrecker hauling off the 55 Ford. My Father was behind on the payments due to being over extended and the 55 Ford was being repossessed!

So much for my brief period of looking like a rich kid. I got an afternoon job sacking groceries and was able to buy a 1941 Chevrolet from Jack Mason for $20 a month.

If the service bays were on the left side, this would be the spitting image of the Mobil station that I ran in the story above! When I discovered this station, it took me back to that fun summer when I was seventeen years old! This painting was published on my 2007 Texas Classic Gas Stations Calendar. This station is at 621 St. George Street in Gonzales, Texas and it opened in 1936 and closed in the early 1970's. After housing several different businesses it was purchased by current owner Bobby Bowden who restored it in 2000 to its former glory. No gas but a standing reminder of the way things used to be!!

HIGH SCHOOL TURKEY

I painted this after remembering a time in high school when our first period advisory class decided to help a "Needy Family" by providing them with a Thanksgiving Dinner.

We picked this family randomly from a list of needy families (I don't remember where we got the list). We all chipped in a dollar and since there were about 30 of us, we were able to buy a big turkey that was already cooked and stuffed, in addition to several other dishes and desserts (In 1959, $30 was a lot of money) .

We had never been to this family's house, so we were unprepared for what we would find there. The house was extremely run down and dilapidated and there were several children that were dirty and dressed in tattered clothes. The Mother was also dressed in worn out clothes. In spite of the sad situation, there was a really nice large color television in

PUTTIN ON THE RITZ

When I was painting this , I remembered the story below from my high school days. This house is near Cross Cut, Texas and the 59 Caddy wasn't there but, the idea is that if you live so far out in the country that no one's ever seen your shack, you can drive to town in your Caddy and folks will think you are a rich rancher!

the living room and there was a late model Cadillac in the front yard.

The Father was dressed nicely in clean and pressed, expensive attire. We were shocked at the lack of priorities of this Father, and wanted to grab this man by the nape of his neck and stuff that turkey in a

place where the sun didn't shine!

Probably, the only thing that stopped us from doing something rash to the Father was the joy and excitement of those children at the prospect of possibly the best Thanksgiving Dinner they had ever experienced! ✦

KILLING THE GOLDEN GOOSE

While I was running the Mobil station, there was a college student who came in and filled up the gas tank of his Jaguar about three times a week. After observing this for about a month I said "you are really burning up the gas, what are you doing, cruising all night or running back and forth to Dallas or Houston every night?" He said "I'm not going anywhere, someone is stealing my gas!" I said, "we can put a stop to that, what you need is one of these locking gas caps I sell here!"

He bought the gas cap and I only saw him about once every two weeks and I wondered if I had killed the Goose that laid the Golden Egg. A few days later one of the kids that hung out at the station pulled in and gassed up his car and it dawned on me, that although he hung out at the station all the time, this was the first time I could remember him gassing up at my station, so I asked him about it. He said "yeah, this guy down the alley from me put a locking gas cap on his Jaguar"! 🐾

PARKED: When I found this old 1936 Ford sitting on the Bubak Ranch near Cat Spring, Texas with a tree growing thru it's roof, I remembered the 1936 Ford that I owned back in High School! The old Ford was in almost as good shape as the one shown here and was popular with my friends because the soft part of the roof was missing and the kids could stand up and look out over the top of the car and wave to everyone as we cruised thru the drive in. I had a tarp that I kept in the trunk in case it rained. When it started to rain, we would throw the tarp over the roof and hold on to it thru open windows to keep the rain out. This worked fine if the rain was coming straight down and not so good if the rain was blowing in from an angle. When it rained hard, I tried to find a bridge or awning at a drive in restaurant to park under but most of the time, we just got wet!

FINDING JESUS!

I was never good with the girls and usually got turned down when I asked for a date. Most of the dates I had were arranged by Roy, (Roy was very popular with the girls and was a fabulous dancer) because I had a car and we could double date.

I liked a girl named Jeannie that I had met at one of the dances held at Hancock Recreation Center and asked her for a date. She said the only date she would consider was for me to go to Church with her, so I took her up on the offer. Church was boring, but at the end of the service she said that some friends were having a prayer meeting at their house and that she would like me to go to the meeting with her. I was convinced that Jeannie was going to be another in a long string of one date relationships, so I was surprised and got my hopes up that our romance was going to flourish.

At the prayer meeting I was asked if I would accept Jesus Christ as my Personal Savior. Not wanting to cause a scene or embarrass Jeannie, I decided to lie (I was still an expert liar) and I said yes! What happened next was one of the most astonishing experiences of my life! I felt like someone had stabbed me in the heart and it was hard to keep my composure. Everyone at the prayer meeting shook my hand or hugged me and they all thanked Jesus for saving me. I was still stunned and after I took Jeannie home, I went home and picked up one of my Father's many Bibles and started reading the New Testament because I wanted to find out who this Jesus guy was.

I got so engrossed in my quest for answers that I forgot all about Jeannie and never asked her for another date (I hope she wasn't hurt) I didn't tell my Father because I felt he would try to guide or influence me and I had a desire to find out on my own. Over the next few months I finished reading the New Testament and what I found was totally different than my Father's hard core approach, I had found Grace and Forgiveness. I won't try to tell you that I was transformed immediately, but for the first time in my life, I felt guilt when I lied or did anything wrong. My conscience had been awakened and I became a not so skilled liar because of this voice in my head that seemed to be telling me I was wrong. I wonder if anyone else has ever been saved by lying. ✦

NOT A GOOD BET

In High School, I was always doing goofy things like throwing spit wads, smoking cigarettes in the bathroom or acting up in other ways that got me sent to the Dean's office. One time in biology class, when we were dissecting worms, I laid my little finger on one of the cast iron radiators used to heat the classroom on cold days, until my finger was very cold and then I laid my icy cold finger on the neck of the girl that sat in front of me and she leaped up and ran screaming around the room, thinking I had put a worm on her neck and I got sent to the Dean's office. I had failed half of a year because I was drawing cars in class instead of paying attention to the teacher and was presumed by many of my teachers to be somewhat of a moron.

I had an english teacher named Mr. Price and I didn't like him very much because he seemed to be the aloof intellectual type, so I tried really hard to get out of his class. Dean Johnson refused to let me transfer to another english teacher's class, so I just tuned out Mr. Price and drew car pictures, deliberately failing the class. Many years later, Mr. Price appeared at one of my Art shows and stated that someone (probably an old classmate playing a prank) had put him on my mailing list and he was receiving my catalog and newsletter. He said "you really do write very well, I know you didn't learn how in my class, where did you learn to write?" I said, I finally saw a reason to learn how and dug in and figured it out"

He said " If someone had bet me my life's savings that you would ever write a legible sentence, I would have gambled it and lost." ✦

DID I FAIL THOSE TOO?

I was in the twelfth grade and I had gone for a few weeks without getting into trouble, when I got called to the Dean's office. I had no idea why Dean Johnson wanted to see me, maybe someone had accused me of something I didn't do. I sat outside his office door in total suspense until he finally opened the door and told me to come in and sit down. He said "Boutwell, why in the hell are you failing?" I said, "school is boring and all I want to do is get out of here and join the Navy". Dean Johnson asked me if I remembered taking some tests in the library and I said, "yes, did I fail those too?"

Dean Johnson told me that he had noticed that I had made an "A" in chemistry (one of the few subjects I really liked) and I was failing the math course that I was required to have taken before I was even allowed to take chemistry. Due to a clerical error I had gotten into the chemistry class without taking the required math course. Dean Johnson told me that because of my

chemistry grade, he had become suspicious of me and had inserted an IQ test into my periodic scholastic aptitude test. He told me that I had scored 152 on the IQ test and I asked him if that was good or bad. Dean Johnson then told me that 152 was about 20 points above genius and that if I had only applied myself, I probably could have been valedictorian of my class.

No one had ever told me that I was smart before and I assumed that if someone with as much authority as Dean Johnson told me so, that it must be true.

I had gotten a previous bad report card and my Father had told me that I couldn't make straight A's if my life depended on it. Armed with Dean Johnson's pronouncement, I told my Father that I could make straight A's if I wanted to and my father told me he would give me $20 for every "A" that I made on the next report card. I told him "I'll break you" and went to school and started paying attention and made straight A's. My Father was proud of me but I never got any of the money. My previous terrible grades kept me from having a grade point average that allowed me to get into the University of Texas, in spite of the fact that I took the entrance exam and scored in the 95 percent level. In spite of not getting into college, Dean Johnson's information had changed my self image and I came to believe I could master anything I put my mind to.

About 20 years later at one of my Art Shows, Dean Johnson stepped up and asked me if I remembered him and I took great pleasure in telling him that he had changed my life and thanked him for the great gift he had given me and on hearing what I told him, he looked like he would break down and cry! ✛

OUT TO LUNCH

I was in the 12 1/2 grade at Austin High School (I failed a whole semester because I was drawing cars instead of listening to my teachers) and had a habit of hanging out on the steps on the West Avenue side of the school after lunch. Me and several other losers, would smoke cigarettes, leer at the girls and make smart remarks at the underclassmen who walked by.

One day, as I was at my usual spot on the West Avenue steps, a "Stunningly Beautiful Girl" and her boyfriend came walking up the steps and as usual we guys did our leering at the girl, however the boyfriend was too big to "smart off" to, so we all just leered at the girl. This gorgeous girl looked directly at me and I was entranced by her beautiful eyes and couldn't look away. She turned her head and continued to lock eyes with me as they passed by and I heard her boyfriend say "who is that?" They went into the building and I just stood there speechless. I'll get back to this encounter a little later, so read on! ✛

GREATEST APRIL FOOL'S DAY EVER!

Since college was not going to happen for me, I reverted back to my former plan of joining the Navy. A friend of mine named Ken Spell was in the reserves and had gotten me to talk to the Navy recruiter and I had decided that when I turned eighteen in a few months, I would enlist.

My Uncle Jim (my father's younger brother) had always been one of my heroes. Jim had been in the Navy, had tattoos on his arms, told stories about chasing Japanese women, rode a motorcycle, practiced martial arts complete with breaking bricks and boards with karate chops and enjoyed a good bar fight every now and then! I wanted to be just like him and joining the Navy was to be my first step!

I had learned to play the guitar and had met a couple of other guys that wanted to form a Rock and Roll band and we got together and practiced and became friends. One of the guys named Billy said he could set me up with a "Blind Date" with a girl that was "really hot" and that we would double date with him and his girlfriend. Billy took me to her house to meet her and when I stepped up on the porch and she came out to meet me, I was spell bound. I guess she did look hot but more than that, she was just the most beautiful girl I had ever laid eyes on and I had trouble making eye contact with her, because I was insecure and thought she was too pretty for a loser like me.

All of a sudden it dawned on me! She was that "Beautiful Girl" that I had locked eyes with on the steps of Austin High several months earlier! She agreed to the date and we picked her up that evening (It was April first,"April Fools Day") and we all went to the carnival. We sat down in the back of the car and when I touched her for the first time, it was as if I had known her forever and finally found her again. I had never felt this much at ease with a girl and found it so easy to talk to her and she seemed to feel the same about me and her beautiful eyes had me in a trance. I had kissed girls before but our first kiss was beyond all my expectations. I was in Love! While at the carnival, we were riding one of the carnival rides, when I glanced across to the carnival ride next to ours and there was Jeannie, the girl who had led me to Jesus, whom I hadn't seen since my being saved. In just a split second Jeannie was out of sight and my attention turned back to my beautiful date. We left the carnival and went to a drive-in for sodas and rode around for a while.

I wondered from the first second that I saw this girl, why Billy had gotten me a date with her when she was obviously much more desirable than his girlfriend. I soon figured this mystery out, when he turned and asked her "where is Richard, I haven't seen him around in a while?" She said "Richard moved to California so we broke up."

It turned out that Richard had been my date's boyfriend and a rather large guy to boot, and this snake I thought was my friend had figured that if I got beat up by Richard, he would keep his distance but if Richard was out of the picture, he would have no trouble beating my time, and he would make a play for this gorgeous girl (I had been set up as the fall guy). Our date went much better than Billy had hoped for and by the time we took her home I was determined that I would go all out to win her heart!

I showed up at her house the next day and she asked where my car was. I was embarrassed to tell her that my 1950 Chevrolet had to be pushed to start and that I had parked it up the hill so it would roll down the hill to start (cars back then could be started by pushing or rolling down a hill) She said "my Daddy's truck is like that" and I knew I had found a real genuine girl (not like those phonies that had judged me as a loser because my car was a rolling wreck) She asked me in and we talked and kissed and talked and kissed and after that, I was at her house or we were riding around in my car to the point of being together almost every waking moment. Billy tried to make a play for her but for the first time in my life, a girl preferred me and she agreed to go steady with me! I told the Navy recruiter that I would enlist when this romance was over, because all of my romances had been short lived and I thought this one was too good to be true. I hope the Navy recruiter wasn't holding his breath waiting, because the romance is still going strong! "Martha" and I were married the following December 22!

As I was writing this story, I realized something for the first time. I met Jeannie at a dance, she led me to Jesus and the next and last time I ever saw her was for that brief moment on my first date with Martha. What if the Lord had plans for me and sent Jeannie to change my life and that glimpse of her at the carnival was an affirmation that her mission was accomplished?

MY NEW FAMILY

Martha's family were poor, her Father drove an old flatbed truck and he cut cedar posts in the Texas hill country and sold the posts to ranchers in the Rio Grande valley. Martha had three brothers and four sisters and was the oldest girl in her family. Martha's family accepted me immediately and I felt like they were my family. My Father and Stepmother didn't like Martha or her family and said they were "White Trash" (my Father seemed to have forgotten how poor we had been most of our lives) and this became more and more of a problem. I had lost my job and Martha's Father offered me a job helping him haul hay for a rancher in Boerne, Texas.

Martha and her family planned to go to Boerne and camp for a few weeks on the ranch while her Father, Brothers and I hauled hay from the fields to one of the rancher's barns. My Father threw a fit and said I couldn't go but I went to Boerne with Martha and her family in spite of his protests. The work was hot and hard and after a

day of hauling hay, I was as hungry as a bear after hibernating all winter. I had never eaten chicken (a hold over from my vegetarian youth) and when we got to camp, Martha's Mother had prepared lots of fried chicken and I virtually inhaled it! (I have eaten chicken ever since) Two weeks later, when we returned to Austin, I found that my Father, Stepmother and Step Brother Rodney had moved and they refused to give me their new address.

I was now on my own. I slept in my car, and stayed at Roy's house a few weeks. Meanwhile, I went to the Texas Employment Commission day labor pool, where I sat in a room with some very unsavory characters, waiting for any temporary job that might come along. The man in charge at the day labor pool said there was a day job, cleaning out a fountain and I leaped to my feet and said, "I'll do it!"

I was sent to a drive-in restaurant named Holiday House on Airport Boulevard and did such a good job that the owner offered me a job in the dining room as a bus boy.

Martha got a job as a maid and we rented a garage apartment close to the Holiday House. I moved into the garage apartment for a month until Martha and I were married. We were married at Martha's Aunt's house and got several sets of drinking glasses as wedding presents. (we hadn't registered with a bridal registry) Martha's Father gave us the best present, he went to the grocery store and bought us a bunch of food! We left the wedding and went to our garage apartment where I carried her across the threshold, and we opened a can of Chef Boyardee Spaghetti, which was our first meal as newlyweds. (we've had Spaghetti on our anniversary ever since but not from a can!). ✦

WORLD'S FASTEST BUS BOY

Back to Holiday House! I have always had a creative mind which has mostly been a blessing and sometimes a curse. I fantasized that there was a "Bus Boy Olympics" and that I was going to be the best and fastest bus boy in the world. I had honed my table cleaning skills to a high level and one afternoon when the dining room was loaded with high school kids, I was blasting thru

the tables keeping them clean as fast as the kids could come and go.

Ralph Moreland, the owner of Holiday House had been watching me in action and after things slowed down he said, "you are pretty fast" and I replied "I'm the fastest bus boy in the world!" Ralph then said, "do you think you could handle the tables at our University of Texas location after a home football game? I said, "I know I can!" He said'" I'll make you a deal, if you can handle it by yourself (it normally took four bus boys), I will pay you double wages and if you can't you just get your regular pay". I was able to handle the after football game rush at the University location all by my self and 30 years later, Ralph Moreland appeared at one of my Art Shows and addressed me as the "World's Fastest Bus Boy"! ✦

Shortly after going to work for Holiday House, My 1950 Chevrolet had cratered and I went To Jack Mason's lot and traded it for a 1951 Studebaker (see picture at left) which was the car that I had when Martha and I got Married. JoJo's, opened in Odessa, Texas in 1959. The Hamburger Roof is about the coolest thing I've seen!

LIFE AFTER HOLIDAY HOUSE

I enrolled in a night school course in drafting at Durham's Business College with the idea that drafting was something I could do that would allow me to use my drawing skills and this landed me a job with Elgin Butler Brick Company and then with Taylor Manufacturing Company in Taylor, Texas. We moved to Taylor and our first child Valerie was born while we lived there. Some of our "dirty minded relatives" had gossiped that, "Martha and I had to get married, because she was pregnant". Our first daughter Valerie was born fourteen months after we were married, but everyone knew Martha had lots of will power and had probably delayed Valerie's birth just to spite those relatives!

Taylor Manufacturing produced institutional furniture for schools, colleges and libraries and I worked doing shop drawings for the installations. A man named Cruz Lopez, who was an Architect,

worked in an office next to the drafting pool and Cruz drew perspective renderings of proposed libraries, chemistry labs and other related projects. Each company that wanted to produce the furniture submitted three dimensional drawings to the Architects for the project and if the Architects liked our drawings they would use our specifications, which gave us the advantage over our competitors in bidding on the job.

One day, when we were taking a coffee break, Cruz was lamenting about having more work than he could handle and he said "I wish one of you guys could draw a perspective". Well, I mouthed off, "I can draw perspectives", Cruz said "show me", I grabbed a napkin and a ball point pen and said "tell me what to draw!" Cruz named one of our base cabinets and I whipped it out free hand. Cruz said, "you do know how, would you like to be my assistant?" I learned a lot from Cruz including producing our company catalog and was on my way to a career in Commercial Art! ♣

WORKING IN THE LOONY BIN

I later left Taylor and we moved back to Austin where I worked for the Texas Highway Department producing traffic survey books that were submitted to the Federal Government to apply for federal money to build freeways. A crew would stop traffic and ask drivers where they were going and traffic counting devices would be placed to determine where to plan freeways and loops. The data would be entered into a computer (the size of these computers were enormous, occupying entire floors in some buildings and capable of almost as much processing capability as a modern digital watch!).

The computer would print out large 18" x 24" tables and our job was to draw lines and borders on the computer tables so that they would be easier to understand. The tables would then be reduced in size and published as the reference section of the survey books that we submitted to the Federal Government.

I worked on several books and it dawned on me that I was drawing the same lines in the same positions time and after time and that there were twelve of us all drawing the same grids all day, every day.

I was appointed to be a "Job Captain" and I had a creative idea and asked the cameraman in the printing department if I could just draw the grid one time on a blank sheet of paper and have him transfer it photographically to each computer table rather than drawing the grid over and over. The cameraman said it would work, so I proceeded to draw the grid only one time and was able to have the entire reference section of the book done!

I was excited about saving so much time and money and was sure that I would get a promotion for my efficiency! Boy was I in for a shock! I was called into the office of the bureaucrat who was second in command in our division. I went into the office expecting praise and was told that I was a trouble maker and that I was threatening the job security of the other eleven people in my section and that I was to never change the procedures without permission again or I would be fired. Surely I had landed in the Loony Bin! I needed the job so I shut up and did as he asked but started looking for another job. ✦

I FOUND IT!

I was aware of Texas Highways Magazine and went to their office and asked for a job several times until they finally agreed to hire me as assistant to the Art Director. Within a few months the Art Director turned the magazine over to me so he could work on other projects. When I started working with the magazine staff, Texas Highways was an internal publication that went out to Highway Department employees and focused on new types of asphalt, new sign technology and retirement notices (a far cry from the great magazine it is today) Frank Lively was the editor and while we were assembling an issue, Frank announced that we had been invited to the press preview week for Hemisfair 1968 in San Antonio. All of the world media would be there and Frank was chomping at the bit to go and hang out with all of the big wigs. Alas, we really had no real business going there, but the idea had me excited as well and I told Frank we should go, I said "they ain't gon'na fire us, we're state employees and besides that, we (The Highway Department) just built a new freeway to service Hemisfair". Frank may have ultimately decided to go, but I like to think I pushed him over the edge.

Four of us (Frank, Assistant Editor Margie Mugno, Photographer Jack Lewis and I) headed for San Antonio and wined and dined with the Who's Who of the world press! I did some sketches, Jack shot some photographs and we headed back to Austin. One of my memorable experiences at Hemisfair was meeting Governor John Connally at the Texas Pavilion. We were going thru a receiving line to meet the Governor and I shook his hand and told him my name and that I was an Artist with Texas Highways Magazine. He must have shook several hundred hands that evening, so on the next day when I was doing some sketching on the grounds, Governor Connally and his entourage came by and he stopped and said to his associates "this is George Boutwell, he is an Artist with Texas Highways Magazine". I was absolutely impressed with the Governor's incredible memory! On the trip back to Austin, we learned, via radio, that Robert Kennedy had been assassinated!

Back at the office we realized that we had some surplus in our budget that we would lose if we didn't use it. We had never used full color and decided to do a color story on Hemisfair complete with Jack's photographs and my sketches. We used up our surplus budget and got accused of wasting taxpayers money and since I was the low man on the Totem Pole, all fingers pointed down to me. Just when things seemed most grim, a member of the Texas Legislature (I don't remember his name) saw a copy of the magazine and sponsored a bill that changed the purpose of the magazine to promote tourism and extol the virtues of Texas, patterned after Arizona Highways Magazine.

Suddenly we had a huge budget and I was Art Director of one of the finest magazines in the country. As a result of the new format all of the fingers that were pointing down at me turned around and pointed up all the way to that bunch of geniuses at the Highway Commission! 🇹‍

Since I didn't have a college education, my salary at the Highway Department was limited and since our Daughter Kimberlee was new born at that time, I was going to need more money. In order to advance, I suggested to my supervisor that I take a correspondence course in commercial art from the International Correspondence School (ICS) and he said, if I could get a diploma from ICS, he would try to slip it past the Big Wigs and see if he could get me a raise. It took me less than a year to finish the correspondence course and I got my Diploma and my supervisor submitted it to the big wigs and they approved my classification change and I was given a substantial pay raise!

I had read an art book written in the 1930's by Ernest Watson that said to do 100 sketches a day for a year to refine drawing skills and I decided to give it a whirl. At the Highway Department we took two coffee breaks a day and I sat and drew people drinking coffee in the break room. While drawing people, I listened to a lot of my fellow employees conversations and many of them talked about having had dreams about what they had wanted to do with their lives but they had gotten "salaried in" and were unable to achieve their dreams unless they took a pay cut and were bitter about it! I looked at that first pay check after the big pay raise and decided I was going to end up as one of those 60 year old bitter guys if I got used to the higher pay. 🇹‍

MY FIRST SALE

In the meantime, while still working at the Highway Department, I had accumulated lots of drawings and paintings and decided to try and sell my Art to earn a little more income. I took my Artwork and called on all of the Austin area Art galleries and two showed interest in my work, the David Gannaway Gallery was run by an Artist of the same name and David, the owner, bought one of my paintings (my first sale!) which he added to his personal collection as his gallery was focused on his Art. David advised me to do anything to get my work in front of the public and was very encouraging. This encouragement helped me get up the courage to call on Austin's most prestigious gallery and my experience there was quite different.

The prominent art gallery owner told me "you have talent but your work doesn't have a theme, you need to do one kind of art like all western, all seascapes, all landscapes, or all wildlife but you will never amount to anything as an Artist if you do so many different things". I said "why can't my specialty be variety?, Your way would take all of the fun out of what I do". There were ten small pen and ink drawings that the gallery owner liked and he agreed to put them in the gallery on consignment at $10 each and if sold, I would receive $5 each. Months later I read about an Art Fair in the park and called and got a booth. I went to the gallery

This painting was the first sale I made and is of an old house that was on my late Brother in Law, Johnny Rainosek's ranch. David Gannaway paid me $75 for the Oil Painting and Johnny commented that the old house wasn't worth $75, so why would someone pay that much for a Painting! This picture is a little out of focus because I photographed it with a Kodak Instamatic camera that wasn't designed to take closeup photographs.

34

and told the owner that I needed the drawings for the Art Fair and that I would bring them back after the show. There were only nine of the ten drawings at the gallery and the owner denied selling anything. The gallery owner then told me that if I showed my work at the Art in the park that it would damage my reputation and that he would blackball me with the "gallery network" and I would never be able to show my work in any respectable gallery (he had sold nothing for me and was threatening to take that away). I decided that I didn't need to be in a business relationship with somebody that was so vindictive and I never set foot in the place again.

I took my work to the Park Art Fair and got lots of complements and made my second sale and several more, totaling a whopping $40! No one was telling me what to paint and I really enjoyed the weekend! I found more Art in the park shows in other towns and began selling more and more Art. ✦

This India Ink Wash Painting was my first Art Fair sale (a whopping $10!) at my first Art Show that was held at Zilker Park in Austin in 1968. I copied a photo from an old 1930's National Geographic article on Greece and made a couple of changes. Later on, I decided to clean up my act and have painted exclusively from my own photographs and original personal experiences since becoming a full time artist!

A TIME FOR A DECISION I had a contest in my spring newsletter to name this painting, not knowing that I would have to decide from over 500 suggestions. This title became appropriate because of the Longhorn having to decide whether to stay in the pasture or navigate the rocks to water and my having to choose a name for this print! This was the first painting that I had a contest to name and the only Longhorn print that I ever published that did not feature one of my own Longhorns. I found this steer at the LBJ ranch!

A HARD, HARD DECISION

Working on the magazine staff was about the best job imaginable but I had decided at that point that my goal was to Paint for a living, so, after much agonizing, I quit the Highway Department and went to work for the Whitley Printing Company as Art Director. Johnny Jones had built The Whitley Company from a one man operation to one that covered a city block and employed about 50 people. I worked for Johnny for two years and he taught me so much about running a business that has been a great blessing to my career.

I had become a member of an Artist group called the Town Lake Art Club and we had a monthly show at Zilker Park and one of our member Artists, Carol Gibson had been taking a workshop from Dalhart Windberg (a famous Texas Artist who was selling tons of prints) and she had convinced him to do a demonstration at our monthly meeting, which she was hosting. After the demonstration, Carol introduced me to Mr. Windberg and pointed out one of my Paintings that hung over her mantle. The print market was in it's infancy at that point and there were a lot of negative opinions about prints in the Art world (still are) and I had bought into the negativism! I asked Mr Windberg why an Artist of his caliber had to prostitute himself with all of those "Cheap Prints". Fortunately for me, Mr Windberg was a gentleman and instead of telling me where to go in the afterlife he told me "You have talent but you need to get out of your own way, before you can succeed. I don't need you to answer this question to me but, to yourself, can you think of three Famous Artists that were never published?"

I pondered his question in my mind for several days and decided that he was absolutely right and went to Mr. Jones and asked him if I could have Prints of my work made an have the bill taken out of my paycheck in several installments. Mr Jones agreed and I was off and running as an Artist in Print! I have thanked Mr. Windberg several times over the years for opening my eyes and being so gracious in the process!

I left the Whitley Company to work as the Art Director for Media Communications Advertising Agency because I had made up my mind that I would eventually paint for a living and thought that working in the advertising business would help me learn how to promote my Art. Media Communications was a hot agency staffed by young creative people and we were taking accounts away from the older, more established agencies and winning lots of awards. We swept the local Addy Awards and one of my Ad campaigns won first place in the state Addy Award competition in Dallas and a silver award in national competition in New York City! An Austin agency had never placed in state competition, let alone the national level! Our notoriety in the Austin Ad community prompted the professor of Advertising Design at the University of Texas to ask our

After thinking long and hard about my conversation with Dalhart Windberg, I decided to make prints of my work. Johnny Jones, (My boss at the Whitley Printing Company) agreed to publish Prints of my work and have the payments taken out of my paycheck in several installments and I was off and running as an Artist in Print! I couldn't afford color prints so my first prints were in black and white from five of my Pen and Ink Drawings shown on this page!

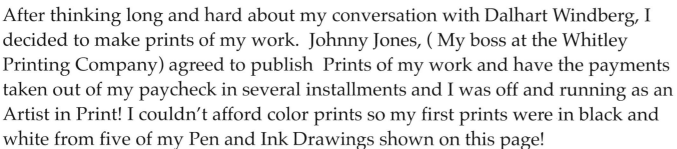

creative team to judge the portfolios of the graduating class. The professor (I won't mention his name because I have no desire to create any ill will) had not checked our credentials and was in shock after the judging was done, to find out, in front of his students, that none of us had a College Degree.

I had always felt a little inferior to Artists with a College Degree and this experience removed my feelings of inferiority! If the quality of my work qualified me to be the judge, I didn't need to apologize for my lack of formal education.

I realized that, it's not where you learn but what you learn that is ultimately important! There was a standing joke in the ad community that the agency that won the most Addy Awards would be out of business in two years and fate stepped in and that joke started to become a reality. We were losing some of our better accounts and the boss was trying to figure out who was at fault, so he fired the head creative writer. The problem didn't go away so he fired me next. By this time I was making more money selling my Art at the weekend Art Fairs than I was making at the Ad Agency so I decided to try and make it as a full time Painter! ✚

Driskill Hotel one of the ten Landmark Drawings I did for the Whitley Conmpany.
See page 40.

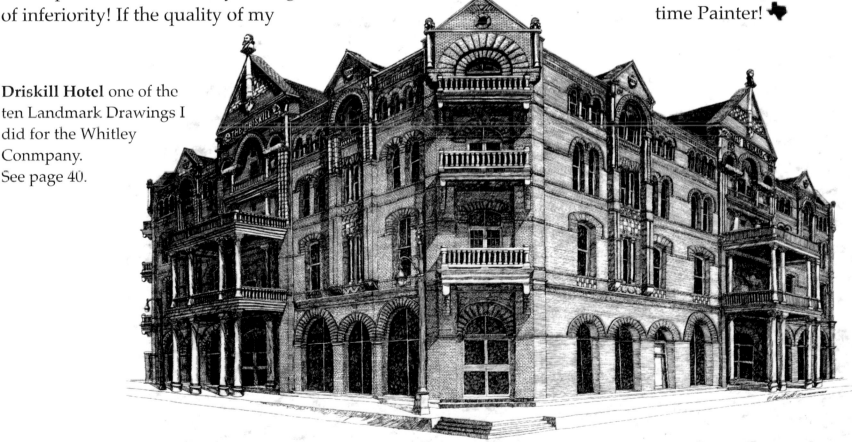

LANDMARKS

Shortly after being fired at Media Communications, I received a call from my former employer, Johnny Jones at the Whitley Company offering me my former job back. I told Mr. Jones that I really wanted to paint full time and on that he told me that he had a project that he would like to talk to me about.

The Houghton House, one of Austin's landmark victorian houses was slated for demolition by a developer from another city. Johnny wanted me to do a drawing of the house before it was gone. Johnny then told me he would like for me to do ten drawings of Historic Austin Landmarks which he would publish as prints to give to his customers.

I agreed to do the drawings, starting with the Houghton House for the sum of $150 for each drawing. I hadn't been to the Houghton House prior to agreeing to do the drawing and wasn't prepared for what happened next. I drove up to the Houghton House and was totally amazed by the absolute quality of this grand house. How could anyone with normal vision even think of demolishing such an architectural treasure? I was so moved by this endangered house that I decided that a mere sketch of this house was not enough, no, I had to document every detail, and ended up spending about ten times as much time on the drawing as I had anticipated.

Shortly after finishing the drawing, the Houghton House was reduced to rubble and construction began on a modern parking garage. Since I had agreed on $150, I decided that I had given my word, so I was committed to do the same style of drawing on the other nine Landmark Drawings!

Mr. Jones was delighted with the first drawing, but told me "you put a lot more than $150 worth of time into this and to be fair to you I suggest that you have limited edition of zinc etching plates made. You can sell the plates to recover some of your unpaid time". It took me two and a half years to complete the Landmark Series and in the process I formed an intense love for victorian architecture and a desire to someday own my own victorian home! Mr. Jones published prints of the Houghton House, mailed them to his customers and I had zinc engraving plates made. I had good sales of the engraving plates due to the large amount of publicity surrounding the demolition of the Houghton House which included an article about the Landmark Series in the Austin newspaper.

I received a surprise call from the developer who had demolished the Houghton House and I found it very difficult to be polite to him. He asked me to sell him one of the zinc engraving plates, which he intended to hang in his office in a place where he would look directly at it daily. He then told me that he had gotten into the deal before even looking at the Houghton House and the bad publicity that he had received had cost him a fortune in lost contracts and that he had learned a hard lesson and would never again repeat such a blunder! ✛

Houghton House

Bremond House

Four of the Ten Landmark Drawings that I did for the Whitley Company.

Littlefield House

Martin Cabiness House

APRIL SHOWERS I owe this idea to a comment made by one of my customers. She said, "you paint storms really well and you paint bluebonnets really well so why don't you ever paint bluebonnets with a storm approaching? I couldn't get the idea out of my head so I finally succumbed and this is the result!

MUDDY ROAD
Mud holes in the road can either be obstacles that block the way or mirrors that reflect infinity. In life, many obstacles or "mud holes" prove in retrospect to be glistening memories that last eternally, because they were conquered or solved and have become triumphs!

A SPECIAL PLACE

Well, it seemed that the minute I was a full time Artist, my sales went into a slump, due to having a rainy May and doing all outdoor shows and I was getting worried. Neal Spelce Advertising, Media Communications, biggest rival at the time, had contacted me and I was doing some freelance work for them. Neal offered me a full time job at a much better salary than I had been making at Media Communications and I had agreed to come to work for him on the following Monday.

The weekend Art Show that I had booked was the Bond's Alley Art Fair in Hillsboro, Texas, a show that I had done for two years prior and had sold an Original each time to a cotton farmer named Ray Sawyer.

I had been set up for just a few minutes when Ray Sawyer appeared and told me the grim news that his cotton crop had been destroyed by a hail storm and he wouldn't be able to buy a Painting from me. Now I

Take out the cars and add some Art booths and this is the view from historic Bond's Alley where I had the show in 1973 that saved my career!

The Hill County Courthouse is a Second Empire Style, designed by W. C. Dodson and built in 1890. This Courthouse was almost completely destroyed by a fire in 1993 and was miraculously rebuilt to it's current magnificent state.

was really worried because Ray had been my best customer and I was thinking that I was not even going to pay my expenses for the trip. Ray then told me that he was born and raised in Hillsboro and had lots of friends in town. Ray said that he had "talked my work up" all over town and that maybe one of his friends would buy a painting. He pointed to one of my paintings and said that he wanted that painting, but he just couldn't manage it. Within minutes a couple stepped up and remarked "this is Ray's Artist" and bought a Painting and several more followed suit and by lunch time I was in record sales territory! I pulled the Painting off the wall that Ray had liked and put it away and by mid day on Sunday I had completely sold out! (the only time in my entire career that I've had a total sell out at a show!) Ray came by to see how I

High Time in Hillsboro
The Texas Theater is just a half block from Bond's Alley and was built in 1926 and got it's current facade in 1940. Giant was filmed in West Texas near Marfa and was James Dean's last movie before his accidental death in 1955. Although James Dean died in 1955, I thought he would look cool in a 57 Chevy, parked between his costars.

was doing and I gave him the Painting that he had liked! I told him that he had saved me from going back to Commercial Art and that I couldn't think of adequate words to thank him! This was 1973 and my total sales for the show were $1500 which at that point in time was a small fortune and enough money to cover about four months operating expenses! I went back to Austin and called Neal Spelce and told him I would not be coming to work for him after all. Bond's Alley seemed to change my luck and my sales went great for the next several years! I am forever grateful to Ray Sawyer and the town of Hillsboro and I told the ladies in charge of the show "If the President want's me to show my work at the White House he had better not do it on the weekend of Bond's Alley because I'll be in Hillsboro that weekend! ✦

Old Corner Gulf
This old Gulf station has been on the northeast corner of the Courthouse Square in Hillsboro, Texas since the 1940's and had been used for several other things until George Herring restored it. Although you can't get gas, you can get an oil change and lube job or work on a Real Estate deal with George.

MY VERY OWN GALLERY!

I found an old closed down laundry on Burnet Road in Austin and thought it would make a good Studio and Gallery, so I rented it for $125 a month and set up shop. We didn't have the money to put together one of those "Hoighty Toighty Galleries" so I decided to go rustic with the decor. I had started making barn wood frames for my Art and had been given several old shacks to tear down for framing materials and I took one of them down and left the walls intact and joined them end to end to create a fence on both sides of the Gallery.

Eric Schmidt who I mentioned earlier from my Boy Scout days had moved to the country and was doing horseshoeing and blacksmith work and came by one day and told me that there was an old windmill that had blown down and he could haul it in for me and we could erect it in front of the gallery. We built a tower of timbers from one of the old shacks we had torn down and we mounted the fan on the tower and erected the

This is the Windmill we erected in front of our Gallery. I did a drawing, then made prints and mailed them out as a Christmas Gift to my previous customers.

windmill. The News Media was all over the erection of a windmill on Burnet Road and we got lots of publicity! I then collected horse drawn farm implements during my travels and placed them along the "Shack Fence". I gathered old signs and nailed them up on the fence.

I was ahead of the curve on the sign collecting craze and was able to get the old signs for free. I've often thought that I might have started the fad of collecting old signs!

Back to the initial "Gallery Opening". We had spent every dime that we had to our names and had mailed out invitations to our "Gallery Opening" and were aware that if we didn't sell a bunch of Art at the opening, we might just have to close it down. Well, we got a lot of folks to the opening but they were just milling around eating the snacks, drinking coffee and saying things like "Good Luck" and "Very Nice". I hadn't made a single sale and I was getting a sinking feeling. Suddenly, a Limousine pulled up out front and all eyes were on the couple exiting the Limo. No one seemed to have any idea who the mystery couple was and I barely recognized A.L. and Mary Scott (two of my collectors that I had met at the Bonds Alley Art Show in Hillsboro). A.L. Scott was a very successful businessman but had always projected a very conservative and humble persona, I had never seen either A. L. or Mary dressed up before! They walked into the gallery and found my most expensive Painting and Mary asked A.L. if it would fit in their plane and A. L. said it would because their new plane had a bigger door (I'm not sure if they had a plane but they were very convincing). A. L. then turned to me and said, "we're kind of in a hurry so can you wrap this up?" A. L. and Mary paid me, got back into the Limo and left.

Like a signal had been sent from Heaven, several people pointed to Paintings that they wanted and proceeded to line up to pay for them! We made enough to stay in business and this was the second time someone from Hillsboro had saved my career. I later found out that A. L. Scott had been on the Board of Directors of the Kimble Museum and knew a little more than the average Joe about Art Openings! ✚

When our daughter Kimberlee was little, she was a frail, sickly child and was six when I saw her standing on a chair, watching snow fall for the first time in her life. A year or so later, Kimberlee had her tonsils removed and became vibrantly healthy and went on to run marathons. When I painted this, we needed money desperately and I sold it to Dr. Ralston Gober and his wife Linda from Corsicana, Texas. Martha really wanted to keep the Painting and I regretted selling it. After seventeen years passed, the Gobers offered to trade for another painting. I gave it to Martha on her birthday and I believe it was the most special birthday present I've ever given her!

This is one of the old farm implements that we found to decorate the front of our gallery. I did this drawing in pen and ink and we mailed signed and numbered prints out to our customers as a Christmas gift the second year that our gallery was in business

DR PEPPER PAINTINGS

One day in 1975 as I was working in the gallery, two men came in and were looking at my work and after spending some time, told me that they were interested in commissioning me to do four paintings that depicted Dr Pepper's four most well known trademarks. The men were Buddy Wall, the Austin area Dr Pepper and Coca Cola distributor and Terry Newton who was an executive with the national Dr Pepper company.

Prints would be produced and given away with the purchase of Dr Pepper in central Texas area grocery stores. If the promotion was successful it would then become a national promotion! Terry told me later that they were originally going to ask a much more famous Artist to do the paintings but Buddy Wall's plant manager, who happened to be one of my customers, had suggested that they look at my work before they made their final decision and that they had decided on the spot to offer the commission to me and had never contacted the other Artist!

Terry and Buddy gave me four vintage signs to use for reference and I got busy on the paintings. True to form, my mind went into high gear and I ended up doing six paintings and they picked four that were all landscape oriented and told me I was free to sell or publish the remaining two as I saw fit. Twenty thousand prints were made and the promotion did very well and just before the national promotion was to start, Terry Newton accepted a job with national Coca Cola in Atlanta, Georgia and Terry's successor at Dr Pepper cancelled the promotion of the four Dr Pepper prints.

In 1983, I published my first set of note cards and one of the cards featured the one with the rooster titled "Morning at Luckenbach." A few years later a man named Harry Ellis with Dr Pepper, who was writing a book on the history of Dr Pepper, contacted me to get some information and when I told him that my favorite Dr Pepper painting was "Morning at Luckenbach", he asked me to send him one of the cards. Harry Ellis called me when he received the card and said "Morning at Luckenbach" was his favorite as well and he included it in the book.

Harry showed the note card to the chairman of the board of Dr Pepper and the chairman ordered a bunch of the note cards for his personal use! The sixth Dr Painting was never published until I wrote this book!✦

These are the four Paintings that I did for Dr Pepper in the story to the left. Dr Pepper published 20,000 prints of each and gave them away in grocery stores in the central Texas area. I don't know why Dr Pepper didn't come up with titles for each. The following page shows the other two Paintings that I did that were rejected by Dr Pepper as well as two others that have a Dr Pepper theme that I painted later.

The Painting on the left, titled "Morning at Luckenbach" is one of the six that I did that was not selected by Dr Pepper

The Painting below, titled "Buffalo Gap Texaco" is one that I published on my 2005 Texas Gas Station Calendar.

The Painting above, titled "Downtown Corsicana" was published on my 2003 Texas Town Square Calendar.

The Painting on the left, titled "Mr. Moore" is one of the six that I did that was not selected by Dr Pepper and was previously unpublished.

OUR PERSONAL GHOST STORY

The Austin Independent School District had come up with a plan to facilitate the racial integration mandate that the Federal Government had handed down. They set up sixth grade centers and all the children in the sixth grade were mixed in those centers. I took our Daughter Valerie to school one morning and after dropping her off, I turned right instead of my usual left turn and found a vacant two story victorian house in the next block. The house was wide open and had a condemned for demolition sign nailed to the front.

I felt strong grief at the idea of demolishing this fine house and I got out of the car and went into the house in spite of the do not enter sign. I felt at home there and went and got Martha and when she saw the house she said that it was just like the house she had dreamed of as a little girl. (She had often told me that she had dreamed of living in a victorian house with crystal chandeliers) Martha had always

MARTHA'S FANTASY
When Martha was a little girl she had a fantasy of living in a Victorian House with crystal chandeliers. While standing in our front yard one morning, I noticed Martha looking out thru the front door glass. The patterns reflected by the tree branches on the window gave the scene a dream like quality that seemed to capture "Martha's Fantasy" that became a reality.

been a little bit psychic and had had several experiences of seeing things before they actually happened. Martha sat down on the staircase and told me how many rooms were upstairs before she ever climbed the stairs and what color the house had originally been painted.

We left and I got on the phone to find out who owned the house. That night I had a dream of a woman named Alwina who told me that we would own her house and not to be concerned with the finances because everything would work out! I started telling Martha about the dream and she finished my sentences. (She had had the same dream!)

I contacted the owners of the house, who were living in North Carolina and told them that we wanted to buy the house and live there. The owners told us that they had left Austin due to the loss of a job and that they had been besieged by real estate developers wanting to buy the house to tear it down to build apartments and that the developers had convinced the city of Austin to condemn the house to force them to sell it. They said they would sell us the house to spite the developers because we were the only people that wanted to save it! We had no money for a down payment, so I called the Heritage Society and asked them which banks were friendly to historic preservation. Mrs Mayo at the Heritage Society told me to contact Charles Betts at Franklin Savings. Franklin had restored three historic houses and made them into branch offices and was very active in historic preservation.

I made an appointment with Mr. Betts, whom I had never met and went to his office. Mr Betts shook my hand and before I got a word out of my mouth he said, "I hear that you want to buy and restore a historic house." He then whipped out a loan application and started filling it out for me and said "I really like your Art work and If you will do a painting of each of our branch office houses that will be your down payment!" I walked out of there in a few minutes with all of the financing arranged. We had to bring the house up to standards before the city of

Austin would allow us to move in and one of the city building inspectors was being down right hateful to us. My Art sales skyrocketed and I was able to pay for the needed repairs but dreaded the mean building inspector when we finished the repairs. We called for the inspection and "lo and behold" a different inspector showed up and had nothing but praise for our work and we passed the inspection with flying colors. I later found out that the mean building inspector was forced to resign due to taking bribes

This is a Pen and Ink Drawing of our victorian house in Austin. I made prints and mailed them to my customers as a christmas gift in 1976

from developers! All during the process of bringing the house up to code, we felt a presence in the house that seemed very friendly and were told by relatives of the original owners that Alwina Lowry's parents had built the house in 1894 and that Alwina had lived there her entire life. She had married the boy who lived across the street and the couple had moved into her house. They had a son, who, upon Alwina's death, had sold the house to a real estate company before any of the family members could even say anything to the contrary.

Alwina had a stroke in one of the bathtubs and her last conscious moment was in the house. The real estate company had sold the house to the people that we had bought the house from and upon the loss of their jobs they had moved back to North Carolina and rented the house to college students. When we moved into the house it seemed to be enchanted and we felt like we had a guardian angel living with us. Valerie and Kimberlee made comments about seeing a very nice and pretty lady in the hall, and Martha saw Alwina several times, always in the hall, but never in any of our bedrooms. I was never fortunate enough to see Alwina (probably due to my gender) but I felt the friendly energy.

Our next door neighbor, A man named Mr. Stubbs, who was in his eighties, and had been a millwright and was an expert on building things, gave much needed advice concerning restoration. Mr Stubbs had built a full scale stagecoach in his back yard! One day, as I was talking to Mr. Stubbs, I took a chance and told him, "I think Alwina Lowry is still in the house." Mr. Stubbs said "I know she is, she really likes you and your family, she made life pure hell for all those other people who have lived there since she died."

Martha had a dream that she was taking a nap and heard the doorbell ring. In the dream, she got out of bed and as she was going down the stairs, she looked down and saw that she was wearing a laced victorian dress with a large pocket on the

front, she reached into the pocket and pulled out a door key with a ribbon tied to it and then she woke up. Martha told me about the dream and a week or so later, I heard the doorbell ring and opened the door to two of Alwina's relatives who told me that they had a couple of things that they wanted give us. They handed me a door key with a ribbon tied to it and an old photograph of a young Alwina and her Mother standing in front of the house and Alwina was wearing the dress in Martha's dream!

We applied for historic zoning to the Austin Historic Landmark Commission and were granted the

first historic designation in the Hyde Park neighborhood and Alwina's house was now protected by law from demolition.

Shortly after the historic zoning, Martha was taking a nap and woke to see Alwina standing in the bay window in our bedroom (the only time Alwina was ever seen in anyplace but the upstairs hall) . Alwina waved goodbye and still facing Martha, went backwards thru the wall and out into one of the trees in the yard, turned around and faded away and obviously went to heaven. We never felt her presence again and felt like we had lost a friend and family member. 🌟

MY BACK YARD These two garbage cans were the ones we used when we lived in the house on Avenue C in Austin. The sunlight cast an interesting shadow on the big dent in the can on the right and I just had to do a Painting of it. I made a print of the Painting, wrote a verse about finding beauty in unlikely places and mailed it out as a Christmas Gift to my collectors which was was met with mixed reactions. However, Texas Governor, Dolph Briscoe wrote me a personal very complementary letter!

TAKING ON THE BIG DOGS

Within a few years after we moved into the Hyde Park house, the neighborhood had undergone a revival and many of the historic homes were being restored and the Hyde Park Neighborhood Association became an advocate for historic preservation. The forces of development that had been chipping away at the historic fabric of the neighborhood, via apartment and parking lot development were now being actively challenged. One of the major problems in preserving the victorian character of the neighborhood was the Hyde Park Baptist Church (Austin's largest church with over 6000 members) which had gobbled up two full city blocks and was trying to ad more development.

The Church had bought the Woodburn house (the second largest house in the neighborhood, the home of a former governor's daughter and the house featured in the movie Leadbelly) and were planning to demolish it for another parking lot. The neighborhood association filed for historic zoning to stop the planned demolition and a long battle erupted. I was vice president of the neighborhood association as well as publisher of the neighborhood newsletter at the time so as you might suspect, in the thick of the fight.

The church hired a law firm to represent them in the battle and the lawyer representing the church got up in front of the city council and asserted that the neighborhood association was just an anti-christian group of hippies and assorted low life, using historic preservation as an excuse to attack the church. What followed his presentation has to be one of the most hilarious experiences I can remember. The president of the neighborhood association came to the podium and said that he didn't quite know how to respond to the lawyers' accusation of being anti-christian and said "My name is Merle Franke and I am the pastor of the First English Lutheran Church" The city council lost their composure and laughed out loud and the hearing went steadily downhill for the church as following speakers for the neighborhood association introduced themselves as attorneys, architects, professors, realtors, a former state senator and other professionals as well as several members of other Baptist Churches.

The lawyer for the church had not done his homework and assumed the composure of the neighborhood had not changed from what it had been before the neighborhood revival started. The following two years saw more than a dozen public hearings which the neighborhood association won. The church had left the house standing open with suspected hopes, that vagrants would burn it down. I had suggested moving the house and had run into a brick wall with the idea because a few influential members of the association were determined to defeat and embarrass the church and had convinced most of the other

Woodburn House, Before the move.

members to stand with them even if it meant losing the house. I considered the house to be more important than the politics of the situation and decided to proceed with the idea of moving the house. The church had much of the political power structure of Austin including the Governor of Texas included in its membership and much of the money to finance the election of the City Council had come from church members. The news media was firmly on the side of the neighborhood association, so you can see that the City Council was in between a rock and a hard place.

I stepped up at a council meeting and offered to move the house and the City Council jumped all over the idea! It took three public hearings to get final approval for the move and the neighborhood and the church fought me all the way! Both the neighborhood association and the church had dug in their heels and were determined to accept only total victory and neither was willing to compromise. I had found a vacant lot in the neighborhood and had arranged financing and at that point the church decided to go along with my plans and agreed to sell me the house for $10 if I would move it.

Prior to getting the final approval I had taken bids from three house moving companies and was in shock at the amount they wanted for the move. I was feeling like I had bit off more than I could chew, when a carpenter that I knew suggested I get a price for the move from a man named Bubba Frank. Bubba had been a house mover in Florida and Alabama before moving to Texas and had a reputation for doing the impossible. Bubba showed up at the site and after introducing himself, immediately gave me a price which was just twenty five percent of the lowest previous bid. I was surprised at the quickness of his bid and questioned him on it. Bubba smiled and told me he had given that same price to two of the other house moving companies who had asked him to sub contract the move for them! Bubba was one of the wisest men I've ever met, he was an old fashioned southern Black man who did all of his business on a hand shake (Bubba couldn't read or write) and was a lay preacher on Sundays. Although Bubba was illiterate he had memorized most of the Bible from listening to others recite scriptures and I never heard him quote anything incorrectly!

Bubba suggested that he move the house in one piece instead of cutting it into smaller pieces and re-assembling it as I had assumed had to be done, because of the size of the house. He said, "that preacher at the Baptist Church knows people that can make that happen!" I took Bubba's advice and told the Baptist preacher that unless we could move the house in one piece, I was going to back out of the deal. The preacher said "give me 24 hours and I'll get back to you!" By the next day we had permission to drop the utility and phone lines which we had been previously been told was out of the question. Some of the people in the neighborhood were opposed to the move and had even gotten a professional engineer to say that the house couldn't be moved and would likely fall apart and if it got to the corner of 44th and Ave. G, it was too big to turn the corner and would fall into the swimming pool at Shipe Park because that corner was on a downhill slope. The press suddenly was being critical of the move and published all of the negatives and were perched with cameras ready to catch the house falling into the swimming pool. Bubba wasn't impressed with the critics and told me not to worry, because he would make fools of them all.

When Bubba got the house to the corner, he pulled the house to the left so that the wheels under the house were up against the corner curb then got out of his truck and poured several cans of motor oil on the wheels under the house, under the wheels of his truck and on the street. Bubba's Father in Law pulled up in another diesel truck and hooked a chain to Bubba's truck and spun it hard to the left sliding on the oil. Bubba grabbed a bag of cat litter and poured it on his truck wheels and on the street, fired up his diesel and pulled forward sliding the house around the corner on the oily street. Bubba pulled forward about half a block on level ground and got out of

his truck and took a bow for the cameras. The crowd went wild with applause and the critics crawled off into the darkness! Two more blocks and Bubba pulled the house onto the lot where it would call home!

Two of Bubba's pearls of wisdom that I have employed many times in my life since those days are "ain't no use for you to worry about something you can't do nothing about" and "worrying about what other folks think will just make you miserable, you just gotta do what

you know is right". Although Bubba was a preacher, he refused to take money for his preaching because he said "Jesus didn't charge for his preachin and if he didn't, ain't no way I'm gonna. His preachin was a gift to folks and I hope mine is too!" Bubba shared his idea of the judgement day which is as follows:

"On the judgement day, those folks will file into that big church and that preacher will be preaching a fine sermon, when all of a sudden, that doggone air conditioner gonna break

The Woodburn house after we finished the exterior and right before we sold it. The Woodburn house sold a couple of more times over the next 20 years and I'm told that it fetched over a million dollars the last time it sold!

down. The brothers and sisters will dig deep into their pockets and put lots of money in the plate and call the air conditioner man. That air conditioner man ain't gonna be able to fix that air conditioner and it's just gonna get hotter and hotter and hotter in that church and that's gonna be what happens on the judgement day!"

Bubba got the house on a new pier foundation and my crew got the house stabilized, painted, sheet rocked and ready to start interior finishing. A couple rode up on bicycles and said they wanted to buy the house. Jimmy Carter was running for re-election at the time and the man on the bicycle told me that he was an attorney for the savings and loan league and that the Carter administration was going to get interest rates way down just before the election and he said "let me handle all of the details and we'll get this done quickly." Sure enough, interest rates dropped like a rock and the attorney closed the deal in a heartbeat. My saving the Woodburn house got me appointed to the Historic Landmark Commission because the City Council said I was the only person that ever took on the church and the neighborhood

association and beat them both! I served on the commission until Martha and I decided to pull up stakes and move to the ranch! ✦

FINDING THE RANCH

Back in time when I did commission work, a real estate agent from Waco named Nat Wofford commissioned me to do a painting of a place he owned on Neils Creek in Bosque County. In the process of Nat showing me the place he wanted me to paint, he asked me why an Artist that painted the country lived in the city. I told him that Martha had grown up in the country and wanted to live there again and that our fantasy was to find a Victorian house on top of a hill with a good view and enough land that we wouldn't be able to see any of our neighbors. I told him, "when

"Neil's Creek" this is the painting that led to our finding the Ranch!

Our house at the ranch, known in Bosque County as "Highview"

my kids grow up, find me that place and you will get me out of Austin!"

Several years later Nat called me and told me he had listed the place that I had described and invited us to come and take a look. We drove up to Clifton, fell in love with the ranch and decided to buy it.

As far as I know "Highview" is the only house of it's age built on top of a hill in Texas. As I stated earlier, Martha and I grew up poor and we were breaking out of poverty by doing the impossible, "Selling Art". One of Martha's cousins had started out poor and went to work in construction and worked his way into contracting and developing real estate and had become prosperous. He heard that we were doing well and offered to help us "Get Rich".

He (the cousin) talked us into buying rental property from him and he managed the property and sent us a check for the profits. This lasted about a year before things changed for the worse. Austin had been over built and the Texas economy went into a deep recession due to falling oil prices and we found ourselves sending checks to Martha's cousin to cover the losses. Things got worse and we had to take over management of the rental property to cut costs and finally decided to move to the ranch because we could rent the Austin house for enough to cover some of our losses.

By this time Valerie was married and living in Galveston and Kimberlee was attending the University of Texas. Our initial plan for the ranch was to retire there after we had restored the house, instead we moved into it with the wind blowing thru the walls and no heat other than a fireplace and gas space heaters. Of course as irony often dictates, we experienced a winter that broke a lot of records for cold temperatures with a spell of sub freezing weather that hit 15 below zero at its low point and we made it thru with a good electric blanket and lots of layers of clothing. ✦

HORSE TRADING

Shortly after buying the ranch I was showing at the Salado Art Fair and one of my customers, named C. B. Hodge, (I never knew what his name was, everyone called him C. B.) who lived in Salado came by my booth and told me that since I was now a rancher, that I should have some livestock. C. B. said that I had a large painting that he wanted and would like to trade for longhorn cattle and horses.

The following week, Martha and I went to Salado to look over his offer and work out a deal. C.B. had done well in life and took great pleasure in negotiating (in other words he was a shrewd horse trader). Martha has a talent for quickly sizing people up and she is a master of non verbal communication. C. B. told us to pick out the animals we wanted and Martha noticed, due to C.B.s body language, that he favored a red stallion and told him that she wanted the red horse. C.B. clearly didn't want to part with the red stallion and by the time we were done talking we ended up with ten longhorn steer calves and four horses (almost twice the number of animals that C. B, originally offered to trade) but C. B. kept his red stallion. The next time I saw C. B. he said "I'd like to borrow that little gal of yours to help me negotiate a big deal or two, I ain't been walked on like that in a long time, She's Great! ✦

BREAK TIME, A tree is a real special place after a few hours in the hot blazing Texas sun and is like walking into an air conditioned room by comparison! This is the original that we traded for longhorns and horses in the above story!

GOING BROKE

The recession deepened and our rental property continued to loose money. The government had instituted a tax policy of accelerated depreciation for income producing property with the intent of getting the real estate and construction business going to create jobs. However when a large number of investors took advantage of the new tax policy the government said that there was too much abuse and cancelled the policy. This reversal of policy created a domino effect that caused the Savings and Loan crash and economic chaos with an avalanche of bankruptcies that even included one of Texas' former Governors. Needless to say, we ended up in the avalanche, but we were now part of the "In Crowd".

The rental market crashed and we were no longer able to get the rents we needed to pay the loans on the property, in fact we could no longer get damage deposits and had to keep cutting the rents and ended up getting tenants that did damage to the property. Our loan officer told us not to worry about making payments for a while and to spend the money fixing the damages to get the properties back to a condition that they could be rented.

We were about five months behind and the loan officer told us that there were lots of people much farther behind and that the bank would work with us and not foreclose on the property (getting some money was better than none and the last thing they wanted was a bunch of foreclosed rental property). Well, no sooner than this was said, the government determined that the bank was insolvent and stepped in and shut them down.

The bank was sold to a bigger bank for about five percent of its value and the new monster bank started foreclosure on our rental property. I had started banking with a small bank in Valley Mills and went there to try and borrow enough money to bring my payments current. The banker in Valley Mills told me that the monster bank didn't want me to catch up because they only had five percent in the property and if they sold it for half of it's value, they would make ten times their money. He said, "file bankruptcy and get on with your life and Art career, don't ruin your health with the stress of trying to cope with fighting your way thru this because it will be a long time before this mess is corrected". He told me that, due to the monster banks position, this probably wouldn't do much damage to my credit rating and that he was willing to loan me money to make ends meet after the bankruptcy.

I called John McNamara, a bankruptcy lawyer in Waco that I had known for several years who had also been one of my art collectors. John sat us down and went over our finances and we told him that we didn't want to cheat all of the people that we did business with. John said "good, I like your attitude, you can file bankruptcy without cheating everyone out of their money, all the court wants, is for you to get into a solvent position and giving all this property up will do just that".

We chose to keep paying all of our other bills and gave the property back to the monster bank (just what the monster bank wanted us to do!) We filed bankruptcy and a hearing in front of a judge was scheduled. When we got to the courtroom there were several cases ahead of us and we sat and listened as people pleaded their cases. Some were angry and loud and others were sobbing and begging, so when it was our turn, we sat down with the judge and were calm and cooperative.

The judge read thru our plan and complimented us on doing the honorable thing of electing to pay all of our obligations except for the property which we had elected to give back to the monster bank in lieu of the debt. When the judge finished reading he turned to John McNamara and said, "John you are slipping in your old age, I see that there are nine longhorn steers that are not collateral for any debt, so I guess they will become property of the court" At that point Martha started laughing lightly and the judge asked her what was so funny. Martha looked at me and said why don't you tell him. Martha and I seemed to be reading each others minds because I knew exactly why she was laughing. I turned to the judge and said, "If you will look at the page that lists property that is in our possession, that does not belong to us, you will find a tenth longhorn steer. The judge said, "why do you

have a steer that doesn't belong to you?" I said, "we traded him for a bunch of hay and his owner has been unable to get him into a trailer. We even hired a professional cowboy who was also unable to get him into a trailer". The judge asked why this was such a problem and I replied, "he weighs about two thousand pounds, has six foot horns and he likes it where he is! At that point Martha chimed in "and his name is Wimpy!"

At that point, after considering what handling the lead steer might involve, the judge laughed and said we could keep our longhorns. He approved our case and as he was dismissing us he added, "If more people had your attitude, I could almost like my job!" ✦

WIMPY:

The painting below was done after the death of Wimpy, the steer mentioned in the previous story and the following is a verse that I wrote for the Christmas gift print we sent in 2008:

Shortly after Martha and I bought the ranch we traded Art for ten longhorn calves and four horses. Just about all animals (we humans included) seem to have a social order, where each member of the group has to find their place. Of the ten longhorn steers "Wimpy" ended up at the bottom of the list and had to wait until the others finished eating or drinking for his turn. I related to "Wimpy" as I had been in a similar role many times in my youth and often gave him some extra feed to make up for his being in last place. As the years wore on and the longhorns got older, they were less likely to shove him around. (I can think of lots of parallels in my life as we all got older) At about 15 years, (old age in cattle years) our longhorns began to slowly die off, one by one until at 22 years Wimpy was the last one standing and became the "Lead Steer" by default. Our other cattle (non longhorns) seemed to really admire Wimpy and treated him with much respect because of his 6 feet or so of curving horns. We expected to find him dead at any time but he hung on for another four years, savoring his well earned position in the herd and making up for his troubled youth. Wimpy passed away at 26 years old and we truly miss seeing him every morning.

A HOSTILE BLESSING

When the Economy crashed and we started loosing money on the rental property, we faced the dilemma of rising costs and falling income. How could we increase our income with falling sales? I decided that we needed a new product.

I was showing my work at the Laguna Gloria Fiesta in Austin, a show produced by an art museum that leaned heavily toward modern art. In a conversation with one of the mean spirited women in charge of the show, I was told that my realistic style of work was not "museum quality" and that it was merely "calendar art". Most of the modern art crowd that I have met have been extremely sarcastic, unhappy, and insulting. I think the modern art must affect their brains or something. Anyway, after listening to her insults, the "idea light" flashed brightly in my mind!

A calendar!, what a great idea!, I went to work analyzing costs and determined that if I could produce a calendar and sell 3000 of them, we could pay for the production of the calendar and clear just enough to cover our real estate losses! If that mean woman only knew what a blessing she had accidentally been to me, it probably would have ruined her whole year! I ran the calendar idea by Martha and she said "we are in financial trouble and you want to spend even more money? We're broke so how are you going to pay for it?" I told her that I had had an "epiphany style creative brainstorm" and was confident that I could pull it off and that I had a 30 day credit account at the printer! I also stated that since we were so far over our

My first Calendar was for 1987 and was a desktop Calendar. I changed designs each year until I locked in on the Current Design in 1990

heads in debt, what difference would a little more debt make!

I said "if I do nothing, we will surely go down the drain and if I publish this calendar, we have a shot at staying afloat" So I announced the coming calendar in my summer and fall newsletters and in my weekly show invitations. I made a mock-up of the calendar and took orders at my shows and by fall I had the necessary 3000 orders and we shipped them out and all but a handful of folks that had ordered, sent us a check and we were able to hang on for another year.

The following year our calendar orders grew, but so did the losses on the real estate and again we sold enough calendars to pay the losses on the real estate. Each year calendar sales went up and real estate losses gobbled up all of the profits. In the spring of 1990, the monster bank started foreclosure and forced us into bankruptcy and all of our dominoes fell! Since the calendar wasn't printed yet and we had taken no money in advance it was not a factor in the bankruptcy. On the way home from the bankruptcy hearing, I had one of those mental "schaza-aam!" moments and said to Martha, "do you know what is going to happen in four months? The calendar will be published and shipped and by the end of the year, we will have all of the profit in our hands and no ones sticky little fingers reaching for it!" The calendar saved our "financial necks" and we were able to rebuild my career quickly! Thank you, "mean art museum lady! "

DROUGHT BUSTER This painting was published on my 1987 calendar and is one of my favorites from that first calendar. My Daughter Valerie was living in Galveston and I drove thru a severe thunderstorm on the way to visit her and I analyzed the visual aspects and sat down later and painted this, my first thunderstorm painting, from memory

INTERESTING BREAKDOWNS
I seem to have good luck with my bad luck

In over forty years and close to two thousand shows, I have never missed a show because of a breakdown, at least never before this writing (never say never).

CORSICANA COINCIDENCE

I was headed for Longview and just as I entered Corsicana I saw one of my trailer wheels pass me on the right side. I pulled up into a shopping center parking lot, got out and ran down the street to retrieve my wheel. I noticed that the shopping center was vacant and that there was a drug store across the street. I walked over to the drug store, went in and asked the pharmacist if he had a phone directory (this was before cell phone apps.) so I could try to find a garage that could replace a wheel bearing on my trailer. The Pharmacist asked me what was in the trailer and I told him I was an Artist and was on my way to Longview for an Art Show. He said, "my best friend has been trying to get me to buy some Art from his favorite Artist", at which point he reached into his "in and out" basket and pulled out one of my catalogs and asked me if I had ever heard of "this Artist". I said that's me! He said, "you've gotta be kidding, really?" He grabbed the phone and called his friend Ralston Gober who just happened to be the Mayor of Corsicana and said "you ain't gonna believe who's standing here in my drugstore!" Ralston Gober said, "I'll be right over!"

DOWNTOWN CORSICANA

DOWNTOWN CORSICANA

This is the corner of 5th and Beaton and Dee's place is the longest continually operating soda fountain in the State of Texas and still going strong. Thanks to owner Dee Hawkinson for his help and thanks to Corsicana historian Irvin Samuels for the names of the other businesses which no longer exist. Lacking photographs, I designed signs that I hope are appropriate!

and was there in about 5 minutes. Ralston and the Pharmacist said they had a friend, who owned a big garage, and owed them a favor or two. They got the garage owner on the phone and told him they had an emergency and needed his help. They put me on the phone and the garage owner asked me about the

trailer and I told him the brand of trailer and he said "I've got wheel bearings for that trailer and we will will be right over!" Within minutes a mechanic showed up, replaced the wheel bearing and had me ready to roll! I then realized that I didn't have enough money to pay the bill and asked the mechanic if he took credit

cards and Ralston Gober told me he would pay the bill and I could mail him a check when I got back home! I arrived in Longview with time to set up my show with 15 minutes to spare before the show opened!
 I will always wonder, what were the odds of all those things coming together so conveniently! ✦

63

SLIDIN INTO HOME This title is from my annual contest to name one of my prints. My main reason for painting this was the dust trail behind the pickup, a sure fire way to know someone's headed your way! The sky in this painting was inspired from my front porch and if I'm allowed to brag, I think this is about the best sky painting that I've ever done!

ROSCOE RESCUE

I was booked at a show in Big Spring and my motor home was in the shop having some engine work done and it wouldn't be fixed in time to make the trip. I hitched my trailer to our 74 Ford pickup that I used on the ranch and headed for Big Spring.

Just outside of Sweetwater the truck started vibrating and after I passed thru Roscoe the universal joint broke. The odds of what happened next are pretty remote but when the universal joint broke, the drive shaft fell onto the pavement perfectly centered and dug into the pavement bringing the truck and trailer to an almost immediate halt. As I swerved to the right to get on the shoulder the drive shaft swung out from under the truck and I was able to roll off onto the shoulder. I looked under the truck and found that the rear seal on the transmission was ruptured and that the differential had snapped into two pieces. Fixing the truck was never going to happen! I noticed that there was a "truck stop" directly across the

highway, so I walked over and went in and asked where the telephones were. (this was in the dark ages before I had a cell phone!) The time was about 6:00 am and each table in the restaurant had a pay phone, so I sat down and proceeded to try and call Mel Prather, (the show chairman) to let him know that I probably wasn't going to make it to the show. An elderly man at the next

table said, "you sound like a man with a problem", I said "yeah, a big one" I asked him if he lived in the area and he said he did. I then asked him if he knew where I could rent a truck to tow my trailer. He said I would have to go to Abilene or Midland, that it would cost about $100. I said "I'll lose more than that if I can't get my trailer to Big Spring this morning" He said, "now let me

SIGNAL PEAK I painted this from memory but most people who live near Big Spring, Texas recognize it. It is said that the Indians used this mesa to make smoke signals, warning of approaching settlers.

understand, sounds like you would be willing to pay someone $100 to tow your trailer to Big Spring" I said "Yes Sir, I will". He said, "I know an old boy who is down on his luck and has a good truck and I'll call him." He got the guy out of bed and said there's a fella here at the truck stop who will pay you $100 to haul his trailer to Big Spring." The guy was dressed and at the truck stop in less than 10 minutes and we hooked up the trailer and headed to Big Spring. We dropped my trailer at the back of the convention center, I paid him $100 and he was such a happy guy, that he helped me dolly my work into the convention center.

I was almost set up when the show opened and still had a few things to hang, when one of my customers said "you're running a little late, ain't

WAGON WHEEL DRIVE-IN Opened in 1949 and was later moved (building and all) to it's present location at 2010 Scurry in Big Spring, Texas. Owner, Susie Roach went to work there as a carhop at age 13 and now she owns the place!

ya." I told him about my breakdown and trailer tow and he said "how are you going to get back home?" I said, "I've got two days to figure that out" He said, I've got a good truck that I'll trade you, for your truck and $700 and I'll go get your old truck at Roscoe. I can pick you up when the show closes this afternoon and let you have a look at the truck.

Meanwhile, Dan Brown, one of my Artist friends, told me I could stay with him at his Motel room, which just happened to have an extra bed. The man with the truck picked me up when the show closed and we went to a place called Huck's garage. Huck was originally from Clifton and we had a long conversation about life in Bosque County. Huck and the man who was offering me the truck and another man were partners in the garage and all were retired oil men and Huck's garage was a retirement hobby for the three of them. The truck was one of several that had been used in the oil field and turned out to be another 74 Ford. I test drove it and decided to buy it.

Huck said they would measure the trailer hookup and put the proper ball on it and hook up the trailer and have me ready to roll when the show closed. I didn't miss a minute of the show, the truck made it home and after 18 years, I still use it on the ranch to feed cattle and haul stuff. Tell me what the odds of all that happening so conveniently are!

Again, I seem to have good luck with my bad luck! ⬥

THE STAMPEDE was built in 1954 as the home dance hall of Hoyle Nix and the West Texas Cowboys. Hoyle Nix, best known for his recording of "Big Ball's in Cowtown" toured and recorded with Bob Wills and was inducted into the Western Swing Hall of Fame. After Hoyle's passing, his son Jody, also a fiddle player, took over as the leader of the band and they perform on a regular basis at the Stampede. The Stampede is in Big Spring, Texas, just off FM 700 on State Highway 350. This painting was featured on my 2009 Texas Dance Hall calendar and prior to printing the calendar, I sent Jody Nix a print of the painting and he said, "now I'm going to have to fix up the place to look as good as your painting."

WHEEL LESS IN HICO

I was heading home from a show in Midland and decided to stop in Hico to have some lunch. I jumped out of the motor home and went into a convenience store and got me a small Pizza, came out and when I looked at the trailer, it had a wheel missing. I hadn't felt anything when the wheel came off, so I had no idea how far the trailer had ran on three wheels. I felt of the single wheel in front of the missing one and the tire was hot, so I assumed it had been a long distance.

I was booked to show at Grapevine's "Grapefest" (one of my better shows) which was to set up on Wednesday and it was Monday. I called Hafford Equipment, a shop in Waco that repaired trailers and told them that I needed a new axle and they said, considering the age of my trailer they would probably have to order the axle, which might take a week. I had this sinking feeling but being the incurable optimist, I started working on the problem in my mind as I drove the 60 miles to Waco, creeping along at 20 miles an hour to keep the remaining tire from overheating. Apparently damage to the tire was already done and it went flat as I reached Meridian, so I stopped and put a spare tire on and continued poking along on the shoulder.

I arrived at Hafford Equipment in Waco about 15 minutes before they closed for the day and I removed the trailer with all of my Art and display equipment still in the trailer. The next morning, Rick Souder called me from Hafford Equipment and gave me the bad news that the axle would have to be custom made and that the other axle was on the verge of going bad and that I really needed both axles replaced and that there was no way he could have my trailer ready by Wednesday. I called all over Waco trying to rent a trailer and had no luck until I called Hafford on Tuesday afternoon and asked them if they knew of anyone that had a trailer with a ramp that was large enough to haul all of my stuff.

They gave the name of a man who they said might have one. I called and sure enough, he had one trailer

to rent and it was just the right size. I went by his shop on Wednesday morning and picked up the trailer and went to Hafford's and totally unloaded my trailer and loaded it all into the rental trailer (about 3 hours of hard work) and headed for Grapevine. While en route, I turned on the radio to find that Hurricane Ike was headed for Texas and would probably end up in the Dallas, Fort Worth area on Saturday (Grapevine is pretty close to the center of the metroplex and the show was outdoors). This news was like throwing a drowning man a rock, but my optimism prevailed. (just a Hurricane, so why worry?) I got to Grapevine just in time to start setting up. I finished setting up by 3 a.m., went to bed, got up at 8 a.m. and got ready to open the show. News of the

DOWNTOWN HICO, TEXAS. This is the corner of First and Pecan Streets and the signs on the buildings with the exception of Howard's Drug Store all exist today. I talked to Bruce Slaughter who worked at Howard's Drug Store in the 50's and designed the front of the building based on his verbal description, hopefully I got it close to the way it was!

Hurricane whipped up a frenzy and the crowd turned out in mass on Friday and I was in record sales territory for this particular show by closing time! More than half of the Art and Craft vendors tore down and left on Friday evening in spite of the fact that those of us with weather radar on our cell phones told them that our area would be on the west or "dry side" of the Hurricane. Those of us that were either die-hards or incurable optimists, (I've always been both) decided to open up even though there was drizzle and winds of about 20 miles per hour. I actually made several sales in the rain and the wind never got very strong. Sunday's weather was perfect and the crowd came out in mass again and those of us die hards, reaped the benefits! (my best GrapeFest ever!). On the following Wednesday, I picked up my trailer with its two new axles, unloaded the rent trailer and reloaded mine just in time to head for El Paso for another show and no doubt the trailer would have probably lost the other axle on that trip had we not replaced them both. If the wheel had come off a week later I might have been stranded in West Texas in the middle of the desert out of cell phone range!. Whew, that was more work in one week than I had done before or since, but again the odds of all of that combined good and bad luck working in tandem to insure that I didn't miss either show are pretty slim! ✛

WEST IS EAST

WestFest is reputedly the southwest's largest Czech Polka Festival and located in the town of "West", which is about 35 miles east of our ranch at Clifton, so in my case, "West is East". Back to my story, WestFest is always on Labor Day weekend and since Monday is a holiday, the festival runs late on Sunday night. After tearing down my booth until 3:00 a.m., I headed home and got there at about 4:00 a.m. and went to bed. Martha woke me up right before lunch and asked me if I had had any problems with my trailer. I said, not that I knew of and she told me to go look at the trailer. I went outside and found that the trailer only had 3 wheels. Somewhere on the way home I had lost a wheel and I had no idea where, or when the wheel came off. I had been just a little bit drowsy driving home and I could have lost a lot more than a wheel, driving drowsy. I travel in a motor home and I have stayed over in West and driven home on Monday morning ever since! ✛

ALWAYS KEEP A SPARE MOTOR HOME

In 2008, when gas was $4 and diesel was $5 per gallon, I bought a diesel pusher motor home because they were cheap. (motor home number 7) Fortunately, fuel prices came down and I ended up with a rich guys motor home on a middle class budget. Well, I now had two motor homes and was unable to sell the old one. I loaded up and headed for a show in Temple at the mall. I got 4 miles from home, when the warning light flashed and I noticed that the oil pressure had gone down to none and the safety system shut the engine down. I got it started and made it to Valley Mills before the oil pressure dropped again and would not allow me to go another foot!

Since I was 10 miles from home, I called Martha to come and get me and we came back to the ranch and I fired up the old motor home and headed for Valley Mills. The new motor home wouldn't move, so I called the local wrecker service and got them to pull my trailer off of the new motor home so I could hook it up to the old motor home. After hooking my trailer to the old motor home, I got my clothes and stuff and headed for Temple.

I got to the Mall an hour later than planned but was able to be set up on time to open. I called the service center in Waco and arranged for a wrecker to take the new motor home to the service center. (The local wrecker was not big enough to handle a large motor home.) The service center called me the next day and informed me that, all that was wrong with the motor home was a sensor that had failed. The sensor cost $2 and the tow cost $1000. I had a great show in Temple! It always pays to have a spare motor home! ⬥

A HITCH IN TIME

I was heading to Corpus Christi for the Country Peddler Show and I was pulling out of our driveway onto the highway when I heard a loud pop, so I pulled of onto the shoulder, got out and found that the ball on the trailer hitch had broken and the trailer was hanging on the safety chains. I was able to turn around and drag the trailer up to my house by the safety chains. The feed store in Clifton sells some trailer accessories so I called them to see if they had a replacement ball and found that the size ball I needed was an "oddball ball" and they would have to order it. I was getting that sinking feeling when Mrs. Conrad said that the man at the auto parts store might have one. It was about 5:45 and the auto parts store closed at 6:00, so I called him and he said that he didn't sell trailer hitch balls but that he owned a travel trailer that had a receiver bar with a ball on it that might work and that he wouldn't be needing it for a few weeks.

He agreed to wait for me and I rushed into town and it turned out that the ball was the right size and the receiver bar was a match for the one that was on the motor home which saved me at least an hour since I didn't have to take the broken ball off of my hitch or take the other ball off of the borrowed receiver and replace it on my receiver bar!

I made it to the show and used the loaned hitch until the new ball arrived at the feed store. One more series of events that seem to be more than good luck! ⬥

FREEWHEELING!

I packed up my show in Round Top and made it to the Giddings, Wal Mart and spent the night on their parking lot (Wal Mart welcomes RV'ers on their lots overnight) I got up the next morning and headed home.

After the two hour drive home, I headed up our driveway and when I got to the top of the hill and was pulling up behind our ranch house one of the front wheels fell off of the motor home! Whew! I could have been splattered all over the road if that had happened at 60 mph. or worse, taken others out with me. The Lord was surely watching out for me that day! I was able to have the motor home towed to Waco and Mike at Midtex Frame and Axle got new front end suspension installed in time for me to head for The Bluebonnet Festival in Burnet! How's that for good luck with my bad luck? ⬥

PECOS RODEO BREAKDOWN

I was headed out to Pecos to show my work at the Rodeo and was cruising along the Interstate, just past the city limits sign of Odessa, when I noticed steam coming up from the engine of my motor home. I whipped off the freeway and popped the hood to find that I had a blown water pump and was loosing coolant rapidly. I got inside the motor home and got an empty plastic milk jug and filled it with water and poured it into the coolant container only to have it run out almost as fast as I poured it in.

I decided to try to find a repair shop and drove into Odessa and at about the time that the engine was overheated, I saw a Cadillac dealership and pulled into their service yard. I was pretty depressed because I knew from my days of running a gas station that replacing a water pump was a major repair job. I was in danger of missing a show if I didn't come up with a quick solution to my predicament. My down mood was intensified when the service manager told me that they only worked on Cadillacs and that they couldn't help me with my motor home. As I was asking the service manager for directions to a shop that could help me, I heard a voice behind me asking, "aren't you George Boutwell?"

I turned around and there was Jack Arledge who was the owner of the dealership and a big supporter of the Stamford Cowboy Reunion Art Show, which I had shown at for several years. In my worried state of mind I hadn't read the name of the dealership. Jack asked me "what brings you into our shop today?"

I explained my predicament and Jack turned to his service manager and told him, "let's get my friends motor home fixed!" The service manager sheepishly said, "Yes Sir". Jack then told one of his employees to call a local truck rental place and ask them if they had a truck with a trailer hitch that would fit my trailer and after determining that such a truck was available, had his employee take me to pick up the truck. Jack told me that the dealership would pay the rental company, (they had an account with the rental shop) to save me time and that I could settle up on Monday, when I was coming back from Pecos.

So, within 30 minutes, I was rolling toward Pecos. I arrived in Pecos and as I was checking in to the Art Show, I asked the man in charge where I might find a motel room and was confronted with another big problem. The Rodeo was such a big event that the only rooms available were in Odessa 75 miles away. The temperature was over 100 degrees as I was unloading and I didn't relish the thought of sleeping in the back of the rental truck or the alternative of racking up over 300 extra miles on the rental truck going back and forth to Odessa. I was bringing in a load of Art to the exhibit hall, when my Artist friend Burl Washington asked me why I was in a rental truck.

I explained the situation and Burl said I could stay in his motel room if I didn't mind sleeping on the couch. I jumped all over his offer! I had a good show, loaded up the rental truck and went back to Odessa and picked up my repaired motor home, thanked Jack Arledge and headed home. I seem to have good luck with my bad luck! ✦

TIRED AND RE-TIRED

I was headed for the Country Peddler Show in Odessa and got just past Colorado City when I heard a thumping sound, which told me that I had a tire slinging tread. I pulled off onto the access road and no sooner than I got slowed down, I heard a loud bang and the motor

The Westerner Motel is at 1201 West 2nd in Odessa, Texas and looks to be in pretty good shape. I couldn't resist "cowboying it up" with pickups, horse trailers and the like! The Westerner Motel is on the Historic Bankhead Highway!

home lurched to the left I and knew the tire had blown. I got out, only to find that I had not one but two flat tires. When the first tire blew, the flying rubber sheared off the valve stem on the second tire (these were side by side dual tires on the rear). Fortunately, I carry two spare tires but changing them proved to be a challenge since the motor home

frame was so close to the road. Luckily I had two jacks and some wooden blocks, so I got the jack under the frame, about eight feet from the blown tires and jacked and blocked and moved the jack closer, jacked some more, blocked some more and gradually worked my way to the axle and got the tires changed. I got back on the highway and headed for Odessa. Just as I cleared the first Odessa exit, the air conditioner compressor froze up and burned up the fan belt (the air conditioner was not even running, which made this a very unlikely thing to happen.) I pulled off at the next exit and barely got into the parking lot of a truck stop before the engine overheated.

I went into the truck stop and got the phone number for the only wrecker service that operated after midnight. I told the wrecker dispatcher that I would need two wreckers, one for the motor home and one for my trailer. I had the wreckers tow me to the fairgrounds where the Country Peddler Show was being held. They dropped my trailer close to the load in ramp and my motor home in the area where the other motor homes and trailers were parked. I got up at 6:00 a.m., unloaded my trailer and set up my show, then called the local Chevrolet dealership and arranged to have another wrecker pick up the motor home on Monday morning

after the show. The Chevrolet dealership got a new compressor installed by noon and I went back to the fairgrounds and hooked up my trailer and headed home.

I no sooner than got to Stanton when one of the spare tires I had put on the motor home on the way to Odessa blew out and I limped it into Stanton and had the valve stem replaced on the tire that had gone flat on the way to Odessa. The tire company in Stanton didn't have the size tire I needed, so I installed the tire with the replaced valve stem and headed down the road. Just outside of Big Spring, the other spare tire that I had installed on the way to Odessa blew (the spares were apparently dry rotted due to being on my spare tire rack for a long time). I limped into Big Spring only to find that no one had the tire size that I needed, so I removed the blown tire and proceeded on three back tires slowly. Just outside of Colorado City, the tire with the new valve stem blew (apparently weakened by going flat on the way

to Odessa) I jacked up the motor home on two jacks and removed the blown tire, then took off one of the tires on the side with two remaining tires and put it on the other side and proceeded slowly on only two back wheels. I stopped at every town between Colorado City and Abilene, but none of the tire shops had the size tires I needed. I reached Abilene at about 9:00 in the evening, pulled up on the parking lot of a tire store and spent the night there.

I got up and was waiting when the tire shop opened. Much to my chagrin, they didn't have the size tire I needed, but they called several other tire shops and found one that had two tires that would fit my rims but were wider than the size that would work on the dual wheels.

I decided that I could have the wider tires installed on the front of the motor home and have the front tires moved to the back duals. I got directions to the other tire shop but when I went out to leave, I noticed that one of the tires on my trailer had gone flat. The trailer tire had a cut on the sidewall and was not repairable and the tire shop didn't have that size tire either. We called the other tire shop and they had the trailer tire that I needed so I limped the trailer over to the other tire shop on three wheels and they put the oversize tires on the front of the motor home and moved the front tires to the back duals and installed the new tire on the trailer. I got home in time to have supper with Martha. Whew! ✦

A COLLECTION OF ROAD STORIES:

SLIPPIN' AND A SLIDIN'

I had shown my work at the Dallas Mid-Winter Dental Clinic and loaded up my show and headed south for Austin. As I was leaving the Dallas area I ran into sleet and then snow and then an ice storm. Just south of Waxahachie, traffic on Interstate 35 had slowed down to a crawl and it took me about three hours to make the 30 miles to Hillsboro. I was exhausted and the road conditions were only getting worse so I pulled my motor home off into a parking lot and went to bed.

When I woke up the next morning, the sun was shining and road conditions were better, so I headed south. The big problems were the bridges, which were still icy, and required extreme care, when I crossed them. The Brazos River bridge at Waco is probably the longest bridge on Interstate 35 between Dallas and Austin.

As I approached the Brazos River bridge, I was following a double trailer tractor truck and as the truck got into the middle of the icy bridge it went into a skid. The tractor ended up in the inside lane facing the wrong way with the first trailer at a right angle and the second trailer in the right lane and my motor home was inside the big letter U that the tractor trailer rig had formed.

I found myself looking into the cab at the truck driver as he was now sliding backwards out of control. I was trying really hard to avoid contact with the truck cab and two trailers which had me surrounded.

Miraculously, we slid to a stop without ever touching even though at times we were only a couple inches from colliding. After we had stopped sliding we were positioned so that our windows on the driver's side of both of our vehicles were facing each other. I rolled down my window and the truck driver did the same and I laugh every time I remember him asking,

"Is yer britches dry?" ✦

BAD AND GOOD LUCK TAKEN TO EXTREMES

I had been showing my work at the Memorial City Mall, Art Show in Houston and my Daughter, Valerie was also showing her Art at the same show. Back in the early 1980's Texas still had its "Blue Laws" and most businesses were closed on Sundays. On Saturday night, we got the motor home packed up and headed for Austin. We were approaching Smithville on Highway

71, when I saw three sets of headlights, side by side, approaching us at a high rate of speed.

I noticed flashing lights from a police car behind the three cars running side by side, so I started slowing down. As the three cars got closer, two of them pulled over behind the first car and I felt a little short lived relief. Just as the first car came even with us, the second car swerved out into my lane and hit us head on. I remember thinking as he was swerving into my lane with about ten feet between us that there was no way I could avoid the collision! At this point I began to have one of the most profound experiences of my life. Time slowed down to a crawl as I watched the car, which was doing in excess of eighty miles per hour, as it seemed to inch closer and then I heard the roar of the crash and was watching broken windshield glass float like glowing crystals out into the darkness. I said to myself, "good, it's not hitting my face" and then suddenly the seriousness of the situation came into focus and I said

"Oh my God, is this my last moment?" At that moment a voice said, "it's not your time." On hearing this voice, I went into a state of euphoria at the absolute honor of being spoken to by what I was sure was God, Jesus or an Angel.

Suddenly I broke out of the euphoria and thought, "it may not be my time but what about Valerie?" I looked over to see her flying up out of her seat, so I reached out and pushed her back into the seat. At this point we slid to a stop and time came back to the speed I was used to. All of this happened in a few split seconds but it seemed more like minutes. Neither Valerie or I were wearing seat belts (the mandatory law wasn't in effect at this point).

DOWNTOWN SMITHVILLE TEXAS This scene is less than a mile from the site of my head on collision. This view is from Highway 71 looking west. I moved the Mobil Station half a block closer for the sake of composition. The names of the business in the 50's were given to me by Elaine Seidel of the Smithville Chamber of Commerce and James Rayley helped me with a photograph of the Masonic Lodge stained glass window above the furniture store.

Somehow, I had gotten my foot on the brake and the force of the collision had pushed the brake pedal up even with the top of my seat and had I been wearing a seat belt, I would have had broken bones and internal injuries! The force of the collision had caused me to bend the steering wheel forward.

I had scolded Valerie a few minutes before the collision, because she was slumped down in the seat with her feet on the dash. On impact she had stiffened her legs to absorb the impact and that was why she was coming up from her seat when I reached over and held her in place.

As I got my bearings and asked Valerie if she was OK, I realized that the hissing sound I was hearing was the Propane Gas coming out of it's tank and I told Valerie, "we've got to get out quickly." My door was a crumpled mess, but Valerie's door looked OK, so I asked her if she could open it but she was unable to. I told her to pull up on the handle and hold it up. I folded my hands together and shoved them at the door with all the force I could muster and the door flew open!

We bailed out and saw a policeman getting out of his patrol car and coming towards us. The driver of the third car that was racing towards us had stopped (the lead car had left the scene) and he and his passenger were cursing us for hitting their friend. I suddenly felt a helpless feeling, "what if this Smithville policeman was going to blame us strangers and side with the local boys?" At that moment, the policeman shouted at the boys to shut up and stand by their car or he would break their *#@*#@ necks.

He turned and apologized to us and said "this isn't the first time something like this has happened out here, these boys get drunk and come out here and drag race, it's really a tragedy"

The EMS showed up within minutes and had to cut the boy out of the car which was lodged up under my motor home. The combined impact of over 120 miles per hour had done so much damage to the boys head that it was barely recognizable. He was still breathing, so they loaded him into the ambulance and sped off for the emergency room at Brackenridge Hospital in Austin which was 35 miles away and the only emergency room in the area at the time.

The policeman took us to the police station where we called Martha and told her we were OK. She said she would call my brother in law, Van Quarles, to come to Smithville and bring us back to Austin. Valerie called her fiancee, Duncan Browne, who just happened to be working as an orderly in the intensive care unit, where the ambulance carrying the boy who had hit us, was destined.

Duncan was planning on attending medical school in the fall and was getting some experience toward his goal of becoming a Doctor. Duncan told Valerie he would give us a report on the boy when he arrived at the ER. Van picked us up and brought us back to Austin and Valerie called Duncan and he told her that the boy's blood alcohol level was two and a half times the legally intoxicated level, two hours after the accident and that his brain was damaged so badly that there was no activity or hope that he would survive. It turned out that the boy who had hit us had been in several alcohol related crashes, had lost his driver's license and was driving a borrowed car.

This 21 year old boy was unemployed, and had a wife and young baby at home and he was out drinking and drag racing. I know the boy's name but out of respect to his relatives I think it would be improper to state it. The Doctors at the hospital convinced the boy's wife that there was no hope and she asked that his organs be donated and life support was discontinued and he passed away in a few minutes.

The tragedy of this boy's wasted life saddened me for months and although the accident was clearly his fault, I still grieved for him and his wife and child. We went to the wrecking yard the next day to retrieve our belongings and the attendant at the wrecking yard said "you are really lucky that the door on the passenger side of your motor home flew open or you would still be trapped in there." I told him that I had knocked the door open and he said "no way" and showed us that the door wouldn't close because it was so bent that it was extending six inches past the door frame. He said "a mule couldn't have kicked that door open, man, you must have had a huge amount of adrenaline running in your veins!"

The silver lining of this story was my hearing that voice telling me that it was not my time. How many people are so privileged to be spoken to by God or one of his Angels and as a result of that voice, all doubt about spiritually surviving death and the fear of it were forever removed from my mind! I'm confident that when it is truly my time to die I will hear that beautiful voice telling me "it's now my time". 🔸

ARE WE ALONE OUT HERE?

As I was packing up my work at a show at the Lubbock Civic Center, it started snowing big wet snowflakes and by the time I rolled out of the Civic Center, the ground was covered with close to two inches of snow.

I reasoned that, since I was headed south, I would probably run out of it pretty quickly, but the snow storm only intensified as I headed south. The snow was now falling so fast that there was six inches of snow on the windshield wipers with every stroke. I now understood the term "whiteout" and was creeping along at about ten miles per hour hoping I was still on the road.

An eighteen wheeler truck came slowly around me and when I could see his tail lights, I reasoned that he must have been able to see better than I could, so, I pulled in behind him and now was able to do about 14 miles per hour. We poked along for what seemed to be hours and I hoped we were on the road and not running out in someone's cotton field, but at least I was glad I wasn't alone out there. Suddenly, the snowstorm was letting up and I realized we were headed down a steep hill and then as things cleared a little more, I could see that we were coming off of the "Cap Rock" and I could see the town of Post below. I was startled to see a line of cars and trucks creeping along, almost bumper to bumper in front of the eighteen wheeler as far as the eye could see and more behind me in my rear view mirror. I'll bet every one of those cars and trucks thought they and the vehicle in front of them were the only ones out there in that snowstorm.

I'm just glad that whoever was in the lead managed to stay on the road! 🢪

TEXAS FANTASY Since I was writing about a snow storm, I thought a snow Painting would be appropriate! It's been at least two years since the last snowfall in our part of Texas but I'm sure it will happen again someday. I found this Dempster Model 15 Windmill between Coleman and Winters, Texas.

GETTING NOTICED AT PORT ARANSAS

Sometime around 1967, Martha and I decided to go to Port Aransas and go to the beach, so we left the girls with Martha's Mother, jumped in our 1957 Pontiac and headed for the coast. When we got to the ferry landing we were glad to see that we were first in line for the next ferry.

When the ferry docked we pulled right up to the front and parked and got out to watch the Dolphins that accompany the ferry. When the ferry docked, we got in the Pontiac and I fired up the engine, but to my surprise when I tried to pull the shift lever out of park, the lever just fell loose, the car stayed in park and wouldn't move. There were two rows of cars behind us and as you might guess, none of the folks behind us were happy. So there we were, blocking half of the cars on the ferry and trying to figure out what to do. After some heated discussion with the deck hands on the ferry it was finally decided that the ferry would have to go back out into the channel

A SHOW OF FINS I'm not sure if this is the same ferry that was in my story but it looks the same. I was riding back and forth trying to photograph the Dolphins that always follow the ferry. As I was watching the fins rise in the water, I suddenly got the idea to load the ferry with 50's cars showing their fins.

and turn around and dock the ferry backwards, so that the cars that we had blocked could back off of the ferry. After the other cars got off of the ferry, a wrecker was called and after about 30 minutes of waiting for the wrecker with the ferry tied up, causing the other ferry to do double duty, causing a long line waiting for the single ferry to move the cars back and forth across the channel. The wrecker finally showed up and had to back onto the ferry to lift the Pontiac by its back wheels and pull it off the ferry. Since I was responsible for the bill, I asked the wrecker driver to just pull off to the side and let me look under the car while it was up in the air.

I quickly noticed that a cotter pin on the transmission shift linkage had come loose and the shift linkage was hanging loose. I got a coat hanger from one of my shirts and with a pair of pliers, cut off about 2 inches of wire, replaced the linkage, stuck the piece of coat hanger wire into the space where the cotter pin had been and twisted the wire so it would stay in place.

I told the wrecker driver to lower the car, paid the bill and we drove off toward the beach.

I worried the rest of the day that one of the drivers of one of those cars we had blocked would find us on the island and take out their frustrations on us. Thankfully it didn't happen.

We drove all the way back to Corpus Christi (about 40 extra miles) to avoid riding the ferry because we didn't want to face the crew of the ferry on the return trip! ✛

OKLAHOMA ENGINE BLOW

I've told lots of stories about good luck on the way to shows and having never missed a show even though I've had several close calls. My breakdown luck on the way home from shows is a totally different story!

I had been showing my work at the Gold Coast Art Fair in Chicago and was headed back to Texas and got into Missouri when I started hearing a ticking sound from the engine. This was in the Summer and the temperature was around 110 degrees. I stopped and checked the engine oil, only to find that there was plenty of oil, so I headed out. The ticking sound gradually grew louder and as I approached Big Cabin, Oklahoma the ticking turned into a loud knocking sound and as I was pulling into a truck stop, the engine blew and I coasted to a stop.

I got on the phone and found the closest Dodge dealership which was about 75 miles away and they agreed to install a rebuilt engine if I could get there. The truck stop had business cards of various wrecker operators and I randomly picked one and called. The wrecker showed up promptly, hooked up and towed my motor home the 75 miles to the Dodge dealership. The service manager at the dealership told me that it would take about two weeks to install the new engine in my motor home, so I checked the phone directory and found a UHaul rental shop a few miles from the Dodge dealership and the wrecker driver said he would take me there since he was heading back home and the UHaul shop was on the way.

I rented a truck and headed back to the Dodge dealership and unloaded all of my Art, display equipment and other personal effects. The chore of transferring all of my stuff was made harder by the oppressive heat and the fact that the back of the truck was higher than the door to the motor home, which required stepping up and down with each item I transferred. To make things worse, the UHaul truck's air conditioner didn't work, so the trip home was a sweaty one. I thought I could find a motel room but every motel along the way was booked up and it was getting late. Finally, at a little after midnight I crossed the Texas line and the first motel I found had a vacancy sign! I pulled in and went into the office, rang the bell to alert the attendant, who came out of the adjoining room where he had been sleeping. He took my money and gave me the keys to my room.

The room was filthy and the bed was worse but the air conditioner worked so I got my sleeping bag from the UHaul truck and placed it over the bed, took a quick shower, laid down and passed out from exhaustion.

Next morning, I was headed into Sherman when I remembered that one of my customers, Skipper Wallace had become City Manager of Sherman and had told me to look him up if I was ever up that way. I called Skipper at about 11:00 am and he asked me to have lunch with him. During lunch, he asked me what I had new in the way of originals and I described my new work. Skipper asked to see a couple of the originals, so we went back to his office and I got the Paintings out of the UHaul truck and Skipper bought "Highlight of the Day", which turned out to indeed be the "Highlight of my Day" as it would pay for the new engine for the motor home.

I thanked Skipper and headed home. I travelled to the next two Art shows in the UHaul and setting up and tearing down my shows was an ordeal, due to nothing being where I was accustomed to it being. I enjoy almost everything about what I do with the exception of all the work it takes to set up and tear down my shows. The average show set up takes about six hours and the average tear down takes about four hours.

My idea of going to Hell, would be, continually setting up and tearing down without ever having a show! The positive aspect of set up and tear down is that the work has kept me in good physical shape.

I was scheduled to do a show in Oklahoma City and my Artist friend Harley Murray had booked the same show and suggested that I rent a UHaul trailer, transfer my show stuff from the UHaul truck and he would haul the trailer with his van and save me some money since the trailer rent was a lot less than the truck rental. I insisted on splitting the gas expenses so Harley saved some money as

HIGHLIGHT OF THE DAY. For some people, that daily trip to the mailbox is their only contact with the rest of the world. I was driving between Waco and Temple, Texas when I saw this old fellow getting his mail; although he must have been aware of me photographing him, he never let me know it and walked on back toward his home. His house wasn't as interesting as he was, so I substituted the one in this painting, which is the Wolf House on East First Street in Austin.

well. We got to Oklahoma to pick up the motor home only to find that the Dodge Dealership had gone out of business and my motor home was locked up inside!

There was a note on the front door of the dealership with a number to call, so we drove to a convenience store and called the number (we didn't have cell phones back then) The man that answered the phone came and opened up the dealership, collected the payment from me and I got in the motor home and headed out for Oklahoma City with Harley following.

Well, we hadn't gone far when the motor home overheated, so I stopped at the first place I could find which was a gas station and I called the man from the dealership and was told that since the dealership was out of business, that I would have to get the motor home fixed in Oklahoma City. He said the work was guaranteed by Dodge and that Dodge would pay for another wrecker to haul the motor home to the dealership in Oklahoma City and

for the repairs. The plan had been for Harley and I to stay in the motor home but we were now having to spend money on a motel.

The Art Show lasted four days and we packed up Sunday night and went back to the motel, got up the next morning, picked up the motor home, unloaded the trailer into the motor home, took the trailer to the nearest UHaul shop and headed home. Harley was way ahead of me and after I had driven about ten miles the engine in the motor home was running hot again.

I stopped and called the Dodge dealership in Oklahoma City and was told that they had replaced the water pump, due to the fact that the mechanic at the dealership that installed the engine had used silicone to seal the gaskets and that the silicone had clogged the water pump. The service manager told me that I probably needed to get the radiator cleaned out and that the dealership would pay for the work since the dealership didn't do radiator work. They referred me to a

radiator shop that was close by. I found the radiator shop and was told by their mechanic that it would take about four hours to remove the radiator and that he had three others ahead of mine. I really didn't want to wait another whole day, so I told the mechanic that I thought I could remove the radiator in an hour and he laughed at me and told me I was crazy. The owner of the shop was listening to the conversation and he chimed in and said, "If you can take that radiator out in an hour, we will move you to the head of the line and fix your radiator first!"

I had done a lot of "Shade Tree Mechanicing" in my life, so I got my tools and had the radiator out in about 45 minutes. The mechanic looked shocked and the shop owner told him to get on it and get my radiator fixed ASAP! The owner invited me into his office while the mechanic was cleaning out my radiator and proceeded to lament about how he was upset with his mechanic and had suspected him of goofing off and how I had proved what he had suspected. When the radiator was fixed, I got it installed in about 30 minutes and the shop owner offered me a job! The shop owner told me that the Dodge dealership was going to pay the bill and that since I had done most of the work, he felt like he should pay me for the work I did. I declined his offer and told him I was really motivated, because I needed to get home. The motor home made it back to Austin with no more trouble and I got home one day before I needed to leave for the next show.

INSPIRATION AND DESPERATION

For years I had seen photographs of the beautiful Beach Morning Glories but had never seen them because I seemed to always get to the beach after the Morning Glories had closed up for the day. I was showing my work at the Beachcomber Art Show on South Padre Island and decided it was time to see the Morning Glories. I got up at the crack of dawn and headed down the beach access road. I pulled the motor home off to the side of the road onto the shoulder in a spot that seemed firm and climbed up over the dunes and found lots of Morning Glories in full bloom. I shot lots of pictures and went back to the motor home and continued down the Beach access road and stopped a

MORNING GLORY I'd seen lots of photographs of Beach Morning Glories but always got to the beach after they had closed up for the day. I was on South Padre Island showing at the Beachcomber Art Show and decided to get up early on Sunday morning and explore the dunes. I found the Morning Glories open and got lots of reference photos and decided that Morning Glory was also a good title for this painting.

couple more times to take more photographs. When I got to the end of the Beach access road, I had a very unpleasant surprise, I had assumed that the end of the road would have a wide spot to turn around, but the narrow road just stopped and there were several cars and trucks stuck in the soft sand.

My motor home was longer than the road was wide and I started turning and backing and trying to keep my back wheels on the pavement, so I would not get stuck in the sand. I was almost turned around and misjudged a little and my back wheels on the passenger side slipped off the pavement and I was stuck!

The Art show was due to open in an hour and I was twenty miles down the beach stuck in the sand! I got on my cell phone and called the Good Sam Club and was told that they would send a tow truck that would be there in three hours! I asked them why it would take so long, since there was bound to be a tow truck service on the Island, since so many people got stuck in the sand. Good Sam informed me that the tow service they used was in McAllen which was 70 miles away! (what a bunch of idiots or possibly a deliberate move to get out of providing service).

I hung up on Good Sam and called directory assistance to find a tow truck on the Island and was in the process of calling one of the tow companies, when one of the Artists in the Beachcomber show pulled up in their suburban and told me that if I had a chain, they might be able to give me enough of a boost to get my back wheels back on the pavement.

I pulled the safety chains off of my trailer and had just enough length to do the trick and within 5 minutes we had my back wheels up on the pavement and I was able to get back to the Art Show in plenty time to open! This was the third time I had called Good Sam with a problem and the third time they had weaseled out of helping me so I cancelled my membership! ♣

BEAUMONT BLUNDER

I was returning from a show in Lafayette, Louisiana and pulled the motor home into a rest area just outside of Beaumont, Texas around midnight and hit the sack! I got up the next morning and drove down the Interstate 10 access road, looking for a restaurant with a breakfast buffet, (buffet breakfasts are much quicker) picked out what I thought was a good restaurant and pulled the motor home and trailer onto the parking lot. The only parking spot long enough to accommodate my "Rig" was right by the only street entrance to the restaurant and I pulled in and went into the restaurant and ate breakfast. I finished breakfast, paid my bill and went out to the motor home and proceeded to back out of the parking space.

My trailer at the time was a small one and more narrow than the motor home and as a result, hard to see. In order to get backed out without hitting a parked car, I backed up about ten feet and before going any farther, decided to get out and check the distance of the trailer from any parked cars. I had this habit of unconsciously locking doors as I exited vehicles, which usually had served me well up until this point! So, after determining that I had plenty of space to finish backing out, I went back to the motor home and "lo and behold", I was locked out of the motor home with the engine running and my trailer blocking the only entrance to the restaurant's parking lot! I had effectively, shut the restaurant down, as no one could enter or leave because of my carelessness! As you might guess, I was not very popular with everyone who wanted to eat or needed to be at work and I assumed that due to their angry gestures, I had better do something and quick! I went into the restaurant and asked the cashier to call the police, (police carry tools to unlock vehicles) to come and unlock the motor home (Cell phones weren't very common back then) and for some reason, the cashier failed to grasp the situation and continued to ring up customers. Not until a couple of angry, stranded men came into the restaurant, shouting, did she look out the window and finally call the police. It took the police about twenty minutes (it seemed like twenty hours) to get there and by the time the officer arrived I was beginning to worry about my personal safety!

The officer quickly unlocked the door of my motor home and turned to me and said in a very stern voice. "go immediately to the nearest hardware store (he gave me the location) and have a spare door key made and put it in your wallet! That's an Order!" I sheepishly said "Yes Sir", got into the motor home and backed out with the officer directing me and as soon as I was

PIG STAND A Flying Saucer has landed and is sending out shock waves! Actually it's the Pig Stand at 1595 Calder Ave. in Beaumont, Texas (now closed and not the restaurant in the above story). I used artistic license and added the wave awning on the left for balance! Pig Stand invented the concept of the drive in 1923 in Dallas! Texas Toast originated at this location and this restaurant has fed Elvis, the Big Bopper, Janis Joplin, George Jones, Edgar Winter, Tracy Byrd, Mark Chestnut and thousands of others!

headed down the street, I locked the door to be safe from any of the restaurant patrons. I found the hardware store, looked around to make sure I hadn't been followed, went into the hardware store and had a spare key made. Now, one of the first things I do when I get a new vehicle is to make sure I have a spare key! ⬩

FLIPPED OUT

It was early December and I had been showing my work at the Pasadena convention center and I loaded up my show and headed home to the ranch in heavy traffic in a driving rain that lasted until I got near Buffalo, Texas on Interstate 45.

One of my least favorite things to do is driving at night in the rain and to throw in heavy traffic, made the stress level go thru the roof! I felt a great relief as I pulled off of the Interstate and headed west towards Groesbeck on dry pavement with no traffic. I drove about 15 miles and at about the time that I was getting

relaxed from my white knuckle ride on the Interstate, I ran thru a dip in the road and heard a loud bang and the motor home lurched forward.

I knew something was wrong and looked in the rear view mirror and couldn't see the running lights on my trailer. I drove about a mile down the road until I found a place where I could pull off the road to check the trailer. To my surprise, when I got out to check the trailer there was no trailer! I turned around and went back looking for the trailer,

only to find it upside down in the ditch. Apparently the hitch pin had broken or had been partially removed by a would be thief at the convention center (I didn't have a lock on the hitch pin) My safety chain had snapped when the trailer came loose. I was thankful that the trailer hadn't come loose in that heavy traffic on the Interstate. No telling how bad that could have been if the trailer had hit someone's car.

All of my Paintings and show display equipment were in the trailer

G. BOUTWELL

BRIGHT SPOT IN THE BLIZZARD This barn, between Groesbeck and Mart, Texas, (close to where my trailer flipped!) stopped me in my tracks as I was traveling to an Art Show. I can't explain why, but I got a mental picture of it in a snow storm and thought it needed the Cardinal on the fence post to brighten it up!

and I was in a state of hysteria. I sat beside the road in a state of disbelief for a while and finally decided I needed to go into Groesbeck and try and find a wrecker. I stopped at the only open business which was a drive in grocery and asked the clerk if there was a wrecker service in town and he gave me a number.

The wrecker driver told me where to park the motor home and we got in the wrecker and headed out to recover my trailer. The wrecker driver put a cable on the trailer and pulled it out of the ditch, turning it right side up in the process while I cringed at the sound of broken glass falling inside the trailer. The trailer box was a little beat up and the tongue was totally destroyed. Both tires were OK so the driver said he could tow it back to Groesbeck. The driver said it was good that the ditch was muddy from the rain because the damage could have been lots worse. The wrecker driver pulled into the wrecking yard, dropped the trailer off and told me I could stay there in the motor home for the night

and said he had a friend that worked on horse trailers that could probably weld a new tongue on my trailer so I could tow it home.

I got little sleep that night, worrying about the broken mess I would probably find when I opened the trailer. Morning finally came and the wrecker driver hooked up the trailer to the wrecker and had me follow him to the welding shop.

I still hadn't gotten up the nerve to open the trailer and when the welder said he could weld a new tongue on the trailer and got set up to do the work, I overcame my feelings of dread and opened up the back of the trailer. I was stunned to find that everything in the trailer was intact with the exception of two large prints that had broken glass. My packing skills had been rewarded! All of the tie down straps had held and other than the two pieces of broken glass there was no other damage to my work! "Talk about good luck with my bad luck!"

I called my insurance agent and he said to tow it home and an adjuster would come by and look at the

trailer. The adjuster came by and told me that the trailer was a total loss and that they would send me a check. I told him that I thought the trailer was still serviceable and that it could be repaired. The adjuster said "you can keep using the trailer, It's just not insured anymore" I asked him about liability and he said that the public liability would still be covered by the policy on the motor home. It didn't seem right but I guess the insurance company had their reasons for not wanting to fix the trailer. So, I got paid for the trailer, did some very amateur fiberglass repairs that were ugly but sealed up the holes in the roof.

I used the trailer for 4 more years and finally sold it for $700 (The original price of the trailer when it was new was $1400) when I had a new larger trailer custom made. I came out smelling like a rose on what could have been a terrible disaster and learned a valuable lesson. I check the hitch pin (now a locking pin) before every trip and have two extra safety chains in addition to the legally required one.

SNOWRISE It was a foggy morning when Glen Sunderman of Eagle Lake, Texas gave me a tour of the area so I could photograph the Snow Geese that winter there. We drove very slowly down several dirt roads that were adjacent to the irrigation canals for the rice fields. Glen told me to hold my door open and when I heard the Geese squawking on the other side of the canal bank, I could get out and he would just keep idling along. The Geese were used to moving vehicles but would spook if a vehicle stopped. The engine noise of the moving truck gave me the noise cover that I needed to get up on the canal bank with my camera before the Geese took off. I was so close that I could feel the wind from their wings as they lifted off. I was taken by the total chaos of the Geese as they lifted off the ground in a disorganized frenzy!

NOT A BLOCK TO SPARE

Most of the stories in this book, happened a while back, but this one happened just prior to the publication of this book!

I was headed for McAllen, Texas to show my work at the McAllen Junior League's, Dias Festivos Christmas Market and was about fifty miles north of Edinburg, when I felt the motor home lurch like I had run over something. The road was smooth and it was close to ten in the evening and almost no traffic, so I ruled out any bumps in the road or winds from passing large trucks and there was no noise like a tire blowing out, so, I decided to check things out.

When I stopped, I was shocked to see that the back wheel on the trailer was missing. The lug nuts had sheared and there was no way that I would be able to mount a spare wheel. I was fifty miles from civilization and there was no cell phone signal!

I decided that my only option was to drive very slow on the remaining three trailer wheels and hope that I could make it to someplace where I could get some help. I poked along at fifteen miles an hour, stopping every ten miles or so to check the remaining trailer wheel.

It took me three hours to make it to Edinburg and I pulled off at a truck stop and checked things out. The tire wasn't hot, so I decided to try and make it to the Mc Allen Convention Center since it was only fifteen more miles away.

As I approached the McAllen city limits, I started hearing a squeaking sound that seemed to be getting louder, so I stopped again and found that the axle hub on the one remaining wheel was hot and axle grease was spattered on the tire. This told me that the wheel bearing had worn out and that I probably wasn't going much farther.

I was about two miles from the Convention Center and decided that since I had never missed a show, that I was going to try to make it there or get as close as I could.

The squeaky wheel got louder with each block, but, alas! just one more block and I would be at the Convention Center and I practically held my breath every inch of the way. Finally, I pulled on to the Convention Center parking lot!

It was three in the morning and all I had to do now was park and get get a little sleep. I had to make a sharp turn to get parked and in the middle of the turn I heard a loud crash and stopped to find that the remaining wheel had come off and the right side of the trailer was now on the ground. I had about one hundred feet to go, so I drug the trailer the remaining distance and parked! The hub, that had lost the wheel was now on the pavement but was rolling, now that the other wheel was gone and no damage was done to the parking lot!

I got up and unloaded the trailer and set up my show, called Camco Wheel and Axle (Very Professional Shop!)) and they sent a crew out and replaced two wheels and an axle right there on the parking lot and had me ready to roll before the show closed!

Can anyone argue, that I don't have a Guardian Angel? ✦

DRIVING IN A WINTER WONDERLAND!

I was scheduled to show my work at Music City Mall in Odessa, Texas and since there had been a severe winter storm and I needed to arrive there at eight in the evening, I decided to leave a couple of hours earlier than planned, in case I ran into ice on the road or other weather related problems. I checked with the Texas Department of Transportation and was told that all of the roads that I planned to travel were open, so I headed for Odessa!

I had driven about 25 miles on Highway 6, when I started to see small patches of ice on the road and slowed down a little. The farther I drove the worse the ice on the road got, but I reasoned that when I got to Interstate 20, surely things would be better because of the volume of traffic that was sure to have melted the ice. The last fifteen miles of Highway 6, prior to its intersection with Interstate 20 were so iced over that I had to creep along at about

fifteen miles an hour. I was afraid to pull off of the road, because I probably wouldn't be able to get back on and the road wasn't wide enough to turn the motor home and trailer around, so I poked along.

Finally, I got to Interstate 20 and the entrance ramp was clear of ice, so I got on the Interstate, only to find that there was ice there as well. I drove slowly for several miles and the ice seemed to be getting worse and the only vehicles on the road were eighteen wheel trucks that were poking along in a long line. The trucks had worn ruts in the ice and as long as I kept my wheels in those ruts I was able to go a little faster.

The ice got worse near Abilene and was about three inches thick in most places including the ruts that the trucks were driving in. There were cars and pickup trucks off of the road in the ditches all along the highway and several times all traffic was at a standstill while wreckers removed big trucks that had lost control and were blocking the road.

I began to doubt my sanity and was wishing that I had stayed home was wondering if my positive attitude had overridden my common sense. (the Show must go on, you know!) By this time it had gotten dark and this just added to the stress of the situation.

I called the Mall Office during one of the times that traffic was at a standstill and told them that I was going to be very late if I got there at all. The assistant manager of the Mall told me that the temperature there was five degrees above zero and that there would be an extension cord outside the loading dock for me to plug into, to run the heater in my motor home and that I could set my show up after the mall opened on Thursday morning.

The traffic poked along for about two more hours and it was now after midnight, but due to the stress of the situation I was wide awake.

I was about halfway between Sweetwater and Big Spring when I saw what was just about the most beautiful sight, clear, dry pavement!

From there to Odessa, I was able to run at normal highway speed and relax just a little for the first time in about eight hours!

I got to the Mall at three in the morning just as heavy snow started to fall and the security guard opened the loading dock door and let me unload. I had decided that it was best to unload before the snow covered everything and made unloading even more difficult.

At around four in the morning I went to bed and got up at nine and set up my show which took four and a half hours. The mall was like a ghost town until Friday afternoon at which time a few stragglers came in, but on the weekend things got busy and I ended up with a better show than I had the previous year! 🤠

TOO CLOSE FOR COMFORT Several years ago I took off from my busy schedule to photograph a roundup, but it turned out to be a rainy day. I was very disappointed about wasting the day so I took a few photographs and left. While reorganizing my files, I stumbled on to the photographs and realized, I hadn't wasted the day after all. I changed the background to one that I thought was more interesting

ONE MAN CRIME WAVE

I was showing my work at Nassau Bay, south of Houston and it was about 10 pm when I got packed up on Sunday evening and after eating supper, I decided to head toward home and at least get north of Houston before I pulled the motor home over to get some sleep (I wanted to avoid Houston's morning traffic) It was almost midnight and I was on the elevated freeway that goes thru downtown Houston when I saw flashing lights behind me.

Thinking it must be and ambulance, I pulled to the right to let them pass, but the flashing lights stayed right behind me and I decided that it must be a police car, so I decided to pull off at the next exit, rather than stopping on the elevated freeway in what was fairly heavy traffic, even at midnight. I drove about a quarter of a mile and pulled off the freeway and pulled over to the side of the road and got out, only to find the officer coming toward me with his gun drawn. I held my hands out and asked what the problem was. The officer replied, that he had been chasing me for almost a mile and that I was trying to run away, (as if he really thought a motor home pulling a trailer could outrun a police car). I said, "I didn't want to risk your life and mine pulling over on a busy elevated freeway and waited to pull over in a safe place" and asked him again what the problem was.

He said that I had a tail light that was not working and that I had failed to signal when I left the freeway and that one of the brake lights on the trailer didn't work.

I said, "did you really want me to stop up on the elevated freeway?" The officer became more agitated and threatened to take me to jail if I didn't shut up and get into the back of his squad car. I have always been respectful to police officers, so I decided that he was obviously a nut job and I clammed up to avoid any further trouble. He did a background check on me and when there was no problem with my background, he proceeded to write me several citations for tail light, brake light, turn signal light, (all due to a single burned out bulb) one for failure to signal when I left the freeway and another for what he said was a dim license plate light. I asked him if I could mail in the fine and he said no, that I would have to appear in court in Houston and he was scheduling my hearing for Christmas Eve!

He finally allowed me to leave and I was so rattled that I didn't think I could sleep, so I drove on home to Austin. I've always seemed to have good luck with my bad luck and the following is another example.

We had just finished an order for several framed prints for an Attorney named Steve Edwards and Steve was to come by and pick up his order the next day. When Steve arrived I asked him if he did any legal work on traffic citations. He said "sure, what is the problem?" I explained the situation and asked him if there was any way to avoid going to Houston on Christmas Eve. Steve said "I have a former law school roommate who practices law in Houston and by the way, the Judge is also one of our classmates from law school." The Houston lawyer was named Jan Banker and I didn't recognize the name but when I talked to Jan on the phone, I found out that he owned some of my work and had received my recent catalog. Jan said, "I will handle your one man crime wave for one of your framed prints and you don't need to come to Houston!"

Jan went to the courtroom on the morning of Christmas Eve and found that my tickets were the only thing on the schedule for that day. When Jan entered the courtroom the Judge said "Jan, what brings you here today?" Jan referred to the tickets and explained the conditions of the violations. The Judge picked up the tickets, tore them up, tossed them into the air and said "Merrrrry Christmas" The Judge then scolded the officer for scheduling a hearing on Christmas Eve and told him that trying to pull someone over on an elevated freeway was not only stupid but a danger to the public as well as himself and the driver of the vehicle, and that if he ever did such a foolish thing again the Judge would recommend his removal from the police force. Jan later purchased more of my work so I ended up making a little profit from the whole episode! ✥

GOOD WILL IN KINGSVILLE

It was about 9:00 in the Evening and Martha, Valerie, Kimberlee and I were headed to the Rio Grande Valley for a show in McAllen and figured on getting to the convention center parking lot at about midnight and spending the night on the parking lot so that I could start setting up on Friday morning for an afternoon opening.

I pulled the motor home into a gas station in Kingsville and gassed up and to my surprise the motor home wouldn't start. I got out and checked the battery connections and on finding no problems decided to go to the backup system which involves an auxiliary start switch which connects a second battery which is used to run the lights in the motor home and to start the generator.

Still the engine wouldn't start, so I cranked up the generator and tried the auxiliary switch again, only to hear the starter turn too slowly to start the engine. It was apparent that the starter had failed and I would need to replace it. Since it was late, I asked the station attendant if I could push the motor home off to the side and spend the night there since I wouldn't be able to get a new starter until morning.

The attendant said "I have a friend who owns an auto parts store here in Kingsville and I'll call him." To my surprise The attendants friend asked to talk to me and asked what kind of engine the motor home had and on my telling him he said, "I'll be there in about ten minutes." Sure enough he showed up quickly with the new starter and helped me install it. I asked him what I owed him and he said I only owed him for the starter. I said, "you interrupted your evening to go to your store and bring the starter and then you helped me install it. I would feel better if you would let me pay you for your time." He said that he enjoyed helping people and the satisfaction of helping was more than enough compensation for his time! He then said "I know that you will think good things about Kingsville" and got in his car and left for home. We arrived in McAllen at about 12:30 and had a lot of time to think good things about Kingsville and this stranger who did a lot to restore our faith in people! ✛

TRANSMISSION AT THE MALL

I was headed for a show at Midway Mall in Sherman, Texas and had about ten miles to go when the transmission in my motor home suddenly down shifted and wouldn't shift back into high gear. I pulled off the road and checked my transmission fluid only to find that the transmission fluid wasn't low but was a deep black color. It was about 8:00 in the evening and I needed to be at the mall in an hour.

I decided the transmission was probably ruined, but maybe I could limp in if I just poked along in low gear. I managed to get to the mall in spite of the fact that the transmission was now slipping and was barely able to propel the motor home.

I unloaded and set up my show and while I was setting up my show, I asked one of the mall security guards if there was a transmission shop close by. He looked up the phone number of a transmission shop that was a few blocks from the mall and gave me the number.

I got into bed at about 2:00 am and got up at 7:30 am, got dressed and went into the mall and called the transmission shop (cell phones were not yet popular) I explained my situation to the transmission shop owner and asked him if it would

REFLECTING IN RED This house is between Kingsville and Bishop, Texas and always catches my eye as I travel Highway 77. Actually it doesn't have a red roof but maybe somebody will suggest it to the owner!

be possible to sleep in the motor home while it was at his shop. The shop owner told me that he had the correct rebuilt transmission in stock and would put my motor home ahead of the other work in his shop that wasn't priority work and that if he worked a little late, he could probably have the transmission installed before the mall closed that evening!

The shop owner came to the mall with a wrecker, picked up the motor home and sure enough delivered it back to me, ready to roll, at about 8:30 that evening! Another story reinforcing my faith in the kindness of my fellow man! I seem to have good luck with my bad luck! ✦

FIRST TRIP TO EL PASO

In 1973, my 1962 Buick station wagon broke down two days before an important show and I scrambled around trying to find a replacement so that I could make it to the show. I found a brand new 1973 Chevrolet Vega station wagon at Capitol Chevrolet for $2300 and bought it.

(it was the only small station wagon available in Austin at the time!)

The Vega was the first new car I had ever owned and I now had the confidence to try some shows that were farther away than I had previously done. I heard about a show in El Paso called the Kermezaar, that was supposed to be a good one and I applied and was accepted, so I headed out on the 600 mile trip. I allowed an extra day to

get there, since I was sure I would be stopping frequently to photograph possible Painting subjects. I was near Fredericksburg, when I saw a sign pointing to a place called Luckenbach and since it was only a couple of miles and I was intrigued by the name, I took a little side trip and found the now famous little country store. (The song "Luckenbach, Texas" hadn't been written yet) I took some pictures but

LUCKENBACH, TEXAS is undoubtedly the most famous country store in Texas and I discovered it back in 1973 before the song was released. You can find Luckenbach on Farm Road 1376, just off of U.S. Highway 290, just east of Fredericksburg, Texas.

waited until 1994 to produce the Painting for my 1995 Texas Country Store Calendar. I shot pictures all day and stopped at Van Horn for the night. I got up early the next morning and inched my way to El Paso taking more pictures of the desert landscape. Interstate 10 had not been completed in 1973, so I passed thru every small town on the way. I checked in to my motel and then went to the restaurant for some supper and was solicited by a prostitute at my table, as I was waiting for my meal (This was the only time in my life, before or since, that a prostitute had solicited me and I'm proud to say that I declined her services!) I got up the next morning and headed for the El Paso Civic Center.

Just as I was about to pass a Firestone Tire Store, I heard a loud pop and realized, that I had had a blowout on a tire that was less than two months old. I swerved into the Firestone store and the technician told me that the tires on my new Vega were two ply and that he was amazed that I hadn't blown them all out in the Desert. Driving slow to take pictures had paid off! More good luck with my bad luck! I had them replace all of the tires and was a little late arriving to set up for the Kermezaar but got finished with about 15 minutes to spare!

The show went well and I sold enough to make me want to come back. (That was 39 years ago and I still come back to El Paso each year for the Kermezaar) I loaded up my work on Sunday evening, went back to the motel and got up early Monday morning and headed back,

WEST TEXAS TAPESTRY This is a view of the Davis Mountains as seen from the north between Kent and Balmorea and is a view I've stopped many times to enjoy. Actually the dirt road in this picture follows the contour of IH-10 and I added the cowboy, horse, gate and windmill. (this is close to the location where I picked up the Hitchhiker in the above story)

taking more pictures as the morning light made things look different.

Not much farther down the road from the scene on the previous page, I saw a bearded hitchhiker beside the road with his jacket wrapped around his head for protection from the hot desert sun and having a soft spot for hitchhikers that stemmed from my childhood days with my thumb out (I had a habit of picking up hitchhikers whenever I had the opportunity), I turned around and offered him a ride.

Much to my amazement, when he got into the car and removed his jacket, his head was shaved bald. He told me he was headed for Houston to see the Maharishi Guru (or something to that effect) at the Astrodome and had been hitchhiking all the way from Canada. Well, the longer I drove, the more incoherent he became and it was getting harder and harder to follow his rambling. He pulled out a pen and scrap of paper from his shirt and grabbed the tuning knob on my car radio and turned it until he heard

a word, then quickly moved the dial, wrote down the word and then turned the dial to hear the next word, moved the dial, wrote down the word then repeated the process all the way across the dial then told me that this was a message from Satan and that he would have to meditate to understand its meaning. I got to the fork in the road that separated the way to Austin and to

Houston and pulled over and told him that I was going to Austin so he would need to get another ride to Houston. He said he would rather go to Austin and try to get a ride to Houston from there, so rather than agitate him, I headed for Austin and listened to more of his rambling. I stopped to use the bathroom a couple of times but he said he was fine and didn't get out of the car.

The Sands Motel and Restaurant is in Van Horn, Texas at 805 East Broadway Boulevard and appears to be doing well. There are lots of Sands Motels around Texas but I liked this one more than the others that I've seen. If my memory serves me right, this is the Motel that I stayed in on my first trip to El Paso!

I decided to drive really fast, thinking it would scare him into getting out at the next stop, but he didn't even seem to notice that I was doing ninety five, so I lost my nerve and slowed down. I tried buying him lunch but he stayed in the car and meditated while I went into a restaurant and ate lunch. When we finally arrived in Austin he said he could sleep in my yard and do some work for me and I finally decided it was time for a confrontation, if necessary and drove to the front of the Salvation Army and firmly told him to get out!

Sensing my anger, he lapsed into the peace and love mode of those days and apologized for upsetting me and got out of the car. The minute he was free of the car, I hit the gas and burned rubber for half a block! Free at Last! I decided that I had paid my debt to all of those generous folks that gave my Father and I a ride when I was little and haven't picked up any more hitchhikers! ⬧

INSTANT JUSTICE IN SAN ANTONIO

In all of my years traveling the roads of Texas in my motor home, I have only had one incident where someone outside threatened my safety. I was showing my work at the convention center in San Antonio and had found an inexpensive parking lot a few blocks from the convention center. After the show, I went back to the motor home and was working on a Painting. The temperature that day had been 100 degrees plus, so I was running my generator to power my air conditioner.

It was just a little after midnight when my generator stopped and since the motor home was cooled down, I decided to just go to bed rather than go outside to figure out

SHOWTIME IN SAN ANTONIO The Majestic Theater, built in 1929, is in downtown San Antonio on E. Houston Street (a few blocks from the parking lot in the above story) and was the largest theater in the south at the time. The movie "The Alamo", was filmed in 1959 at Brackettville, Texas and seemed appropriate, since the real Alamo is just a few blocks away!

why the generator had quit, besides I figured that it would stay cool in the motor home until morning.

Suddenly, I heard something bump against the motor home, so I got in the drivers seat and pulled the curtain aside too see what had made the noise. To my surprise, there was a man standing there by the drivers side door and he didn't look like a nice guy!

I lowered the window about half an inch and asked him what he wanted. He said, "you see that man over there? (pointing to the front of the motor home), He's Crazy, Craaazy". The man was about ten feet in front of the motor home with his back to me and he was bent over with his arms dangling motionless. I didn't feel safe and since I always keep my keys in the ignition switch, I fired up the engine and drove off!

I drove to the loading dock of the Convention Center and told the security guard what had happened and he said it would be OK to park there for the rest of the night as long as I left the dock before 8:00 in the morning. (I had done several shows at the convention center and knew the security guard pretty well) I got up the next morning, drove back to the parking lot and as I was pulling into my spot I noticed that the service door to my refrigerator was laying on the ground. I got out to pick it up and noticed that the service door to my generator was hanging open and the screw-in oil filler cap was laying on the ground and there was oil sprayed along the side of the motor home.

Those two men had apparently intended to rob me by shutting down my generator, in order to get me to exit the motor home, but fate had stepped in and foiled their plan. The generator was equipped with a switch that shut the engine down when the oil pressure dropped. What had happened was, the man had not seen the "kill switch" on the generator and had instead, decided to unscrew the pressurized oil filler cap, which resulted in four quarts of boiling oil being sprayed in his face and then deflecting off of him and spraying the side of the motor home. He then apparently staggered out in front of the motor home and was bent over in agony, from what were certainly third degree burns all over his face and upper body. That's why his buddy was saying "That Man is Craaazy" I'll bet that pair never has bothered another motor home! ✦

PLAYING THE PIANO BRIDGE

I had heard about the old Church at Dubina, Texas and decided that I needed to go there and shoot pictures of it, since I was working on my 1997 Country Church Calendar! The Church at Dubina is located on a dirt road and after I took my pictures, I checked my county maps and it showed that the dirt road went west to intersect with U. S. Highway 77, which was the road that I needed to be on to get home.

I decided to stay on the dirt road, since taking it would save me several miles and I like back roads for the possible painting ideas that might appear! Well, the farther I went down that road, the narrower it became and after driving about a mile, I came to an ancient bridge crossing the Navidad River. The sign by the bridge said "Load Limit 9000 Pounds" which presented a big problem, since my motor home and trailer weighed nearly twice the weight limit!

The thought of backing the motor home and trailer nearly a mile on that narrow road was daunting, so I got out and went under the bridge and inspected it to determine it's soundness. The structural beams of the bridge were 12" thick and the roadbed was made of railroad ties so I decided that it should easily hold up if I drove across it.

I got up my nerve and started across the bridge and each plank that I drove across made a pinging sound as the plank bounced on the steel frame and I realized that the planks were loose and moving up and down. I broke out in a sweat and fear gripped me, as I slowly crawled across the bridge. "What if the whole thing collapsed? How would I ever get out of this predicament?" I really thought I had made a huge mistake! Finally, after what seemed an eternity, I was over the bridge and back on solid ground!

Several weeks later at one of my shows, I was showing the Dubina Church Original and I had a conversation with a man who was from the Weimar area and he told me that the local folks in the area called that bridge "The Piano Bridge" because of the tunes it played when a vehicle crossed it! ⬥

DUBINA TEXAS, which means Oak Grove in Czech, is located on FM 1383 Northwest of Weimar and was the first Czech settlement in Texas. St. Cyril and Methodius Catholic Church was rebuilt in 1912 after a hurricane destroyed the original Church and much of the town in 1909.

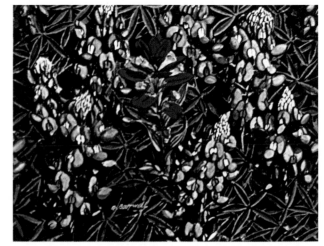

A BUNCH OF ART SHOW STORIES:

AN EXPENSIVE SWEATER

Early in my Art Show career, I joined a group of Artists called the Town Lake Art Club and we would go out to Zilker Park in Austin and set up our Art under a grove of Pecan trees that was beside the road and very visible to passers by. We were later given the opportunity to have a show, at what was at the time, a new and prominent shopping center called Capital Plaza and decided that we would give it a try.

My space was under the front overhang of the Montgomery Ward store and I had placed my wire easels along the street side of the overhang between two columns. I had been showing my work to passers by for a couple of hours, when a man wearing a sweater came out of the store with the Montgomery Ward's store detective following behind him. As they approached my Art Show, the store detective tapped the man on the shoulder and said "I'll take the sweater". As the man with the sweater turned around he pulled a knife from his pocket and slashed the store detective across the forehead leaving a nasty gash.

The store detective apparently had had some kind of combat training, because without hesitation to assess his wound, he said "nobody cuts me" as he kicked the shoplifter in the chest with such force that the shoplifter actually left the ground and slammed into the brick wall of the store building.

The shoplifter was unconscious when he slid down the wall and slumped to the floor, as the store detective who was bleeding profusely, proceeded to kick him several times and then to kneel down and beat the shoplifter with his fists, until the Police arrived and pulled him off of the shoplifter. An ambulance arrived almost instantly and began loading the unconscious shoplifter, who was still wearing the now very bloody sweater, on to a gurney.

The store detective who was now being held back by the Police kept saying, "nobody cuts me" until he passed out from loss of blood and had to be loaded into the ambulance side by side with the shoplifter.

The Montgomery Ward maintenance crew came out and cleaned up the blood and things went back to normal (sort of). As we were closing, I asked one of the Montgomery Ward employees if there was any news on the condition of the store detective and was told that, other than some stitches and a blood transfusion, the detective was doing fine but the shoplifter was in a coma. Thus ended my first shopping center Art Show and none since have been quite that exciting! ✦

YOU CAN'T JUDGE A BOOK BY IT'S COVER!

I was showing my work at the Bond's Alley Arts and Craft Fair in Hillsboro on a hot June day and noticed a man who looked like one of the homeless folks that we are all familiar with. He was dirty, had messy, oily hair, several days beard growth and his clothes were filthy. As I watched him approaching, I noticed that every Artist that he passed, refused to make eye contact with him and made great efforts to avoid him. There was something about him that seemed to be a contradiction.

Most homeless people appear to be depressed and slouch along looking down but this guy was walking upright and he had a little grin on his face, maybe he was just plain crazy, but I couldn't help being curious. As he came to my booth, I made eye contact with him and said "how are you today?" He replied "I'm doing just great" and stepped into my booth. His body odor was really bad but I was still curious so I kept paying attention to him. He looked closely at each Painting and commented that I had really good design and color use in my work. He then pointed to one of my Originals and said "I collect Art and I want to add this painting to my collection".

He reached into his front pants pocket and pulled out a roll of cash and peeled off eight one hundred dollar bills! I asked him for his name and address for my mailing list and he said, "I'll bet you'd also like an explanation as to why I'm so trashed out!" At which point he told me that he was a Surgeon from Houston and had been on a fishing and camping trip at Lake Whitney which is not far from Hillsboro. He said "I came up here with a bunch of buddies to fish and escape for a couple of weeks. We are all successful guys that work in high pressure fields and we've been acting like a bunch of kids. We made a pact that the first guy that changed clothes, shaved or bathed had to pay for all the beer. My buddies know I collect Art so they "double dog dared" me to come to the Art show looking like a dirty bum. I can't think of when I've had more fun. In Houston I'm always being hit on by people to invest in some deal or donate my services and it's been a blast to walk around in public and be ignored!" ⬤

THEM TIRE TRACKS IS REAL!

I was showing my work at Bon Marche Mall in Baton Rouge Louisiana and had two Originals that I was going to publish as Limited Edition Prints later in the year. I had sold both of the Paintings but needed to keep them until the Prints were made so that I could take orders and to have the Paintings to compare to the prints in the pressroom. I was being very careful with the Paintings and removed them from my show each evening when the Mall closed and put them in the motor home for security.

On Saturday evening, I put the Originals on a flat dolly and hauled them out to the motor home. I had the dolly beside the door of the motor home and had picked up the first Painting and was putting it away when I heard a pickup truck coming by and heard breaking glass.

I jumped to the door and there was this truck which had just ran over the Original that was still on the dolly. The driver had an entire empty parking lot but had drove within two feet of my motor home and ran over the Painting! To make things worse the driver was being verbally abusive and asked why the "Damn Painting" was in his way. I determined that he was "drunk as a skunk" and I was lucky he hadn't hit the motor home. Before I could ask for his name, address and insurance info, he jumped in the truck and burned rubber across the parking lot.

I wrote down his license plate number, picked up what was left of the Painting and went back into the Mall and called the Police. (cell phones weren't available back then so I had to use a pay phone) The Police came out and said that there was nothing they could do but filed a report so that I could get the

drivers name from their database. I called the driver and he denied ever being anywhere near the Mall. (probably too drunk to know where he had been). I called the owner of

the Painting with the bad news and told him that I would try to restore the Painting and if I couldn't, I would refund his money (I didn't have the money). I spent more time

WAITING FOR THE BUS This is the painting that got run over in the story above. A dog seems to have an internal clock to tell him important things, like when to wait for the school bus and greet the children. This road is in the Texas Panhandle near Pampa and the dog lived in our neighborhood in Austin and knew just when to wait for Martha and I to pet him as we took our daily walk!

fixing the Painting and repainting missing pieces than I spent doing the Painting to begin with but it turned out really good and the owner of the Painting was happy. He said it would be worth more to him because of the extra time I had put into it and that he would have fun telling his friends that the "Tire Tracks" in the Painting were real! ✦

WHEN ROOT BEER, WAS BOOT BEER

I was showing my Artwork at Sunset Mall in San Angelo and since it was lunch time, I decided to go down the mall to the Taco Bell and get some lunch. I got my food to go because I don't like to leave my show for any longer than I have to because I don't want to miss that big customer!

Well, as I was waiting for my food, I realized that I needed to visit the rest room which was on the way back to my Art Show. So, I took my food which included a large cup of

Root Beer and headed for the rest room. I entered the rest room, got into a stall and since I didn't want to put my food on the floor of a public rest room, (no telling what might be on that floor) I placed the big Root Beer cup on the toilet paper dispenser and hung the plastic bag with my food on the door latch.

Just as I was finishing my business, some guy entered the stall next to mine and bumped into the wall of the stall, knocking the big cup of Root Beer off of the paper dispenser, making it land squarely between my knees, dumping it's contents into my underwear and pants and filling both of my cowboy boots with ice and Root Beer. I sat there stunned for a couple of seconds and then started laughing. The humor of the situation was too good to ignore. Fortunately the hall to the right of the rest room at Sunset Mall goes to the outdoor service and loading area and I was able to sneak out without being seen and went to my motor home and changed clothes. I did empty my boots before leaving the stall. ✦

PUTTING IT ALL IN ONE SENTENCE!

I was showing at a parking lot show at Nassau Bay, across the road from the NASA Space Center (I'm not sure if there is any connection to the synonymous sounds of NASA and Nassau) There was an Artist on the circuit at the time who was like the cartoon character in Little Abner with the rain cloud over his head. All this Artist, who, in spite of his attitude, did excellent work, seemed to do was complain about everything and be obsessed with doom and gloom and always was saying "there's gotta be a better way than this to make money". There was a young woman, photographer who was trying to break into the "Art Biz" and after coming to several shows and picking the brains of us full timers, had finally gotten the nerve to set up at her first show.
I had to leave my booth for some "nature stuff" and as I was returning to my booth, I passed the young photographer lady's booth and there was "Mr. Doom and

Gloom" telling her all of the negatives. She stopped me and asked, "is it really as bad as he says?" Somehow words spilled out of my mouth that were sheer genius (probably from God since I'm not usually so articulate) I said, "I love what I do, I like to travel, I go to interesting places, meet really nice people who tell me I'm wonderful and give me money, I don't know how things could be any better!" Mr. Doom and Gloom glared me as if to say, "how dare you be so positive" and slumped away to his booth.

Every time I start getting a bad attitude at a show, I repeat that statement to myself until the bad attitude crawls back under a rock! I have been truly blessed! ✛

SPELLBOUND AT THE MALL

I was showing my work in Houston at the Memorial City Mall and had just finished a small painting that was quite simple. The painting was simply a white wooden gate. I was talking to Perry Vick,

who had collected my work for several years, when a woman walked up to the gate painting and broke down and began to cry. I asked her if there was something we could do for her and after several minutes of crying she gained her composure and related that her husband had recently passed away and somehow that gate symbolized her plight, as if her husband was on the other side of the gate and she was unable to pass thru the gate. She introduced herself as Martha Ripple,

then turned and slowly walked away looking back at the painting as she left.

Perry Vick was amazed at her strong reaction and decided that since the painting had special energy, that he would purchase it. Memorial City Mall had Art Shows quarterly and at the next show Perry Vick and Martha Ripple both arrived at the same time walking in from opposite directions. Martha asked me if I still had the gate painting and I told her that Perry had purchased it. Perry offered to go home and bring the

This is the Gate Painting that is the subject of the story above. I photographed this Painting with the glass still on it, on the day that it sold. That's why this image is a little fuzzy, but that just makes it more mysterious looking..

painting to the Mall for her to see but she said that it wouldn't be necessary. At the next quarterly show at Memorial Mall, Perry and Martha both walked up from different directions at the same time again and Perry made the same offer to show her the painting. For the next two years, Perry and Martha showed up simultaneously each time. This happened eight consecutive times! Finally Martha showed up and Perry didn't and I was a little relieved as these coincidences were beginning to be so incredibly strange. Martha told me that she had met a wonderful man who had proposed marriage and that she had accepted his offer.

Martha had been gone less than half an hour, when Perry showed up and said that he was surprised that Martha wasn't there. I told him about her coming marriage and he was relieved and glad that she was finally finding happiness and that the spell of the Gate Painting had finally released her. Now you might think that Perry and Martha might

have been communicating their arrival times to each other just to weird me out or that there was something predestined for Perry and Martha to have a romantic relationship but since Martha was much older than Perry, I doubt that was the case. ♣

WHAT IS QUALITY TIME?

As I began to do more Art Shows, I bought a motor home which allowed me to have a place to sleep when I was on the road and I now had room to take Martha and our two daughters Valerie and Kimberlee with me. We would head out right after school was out, do a weekend Art Show and get back to Austin in time for the girls to be in school on Monday. I was told by well meaning friends and relatives, that I was making a big mistake by dragging my kids off to Art Shows every weekend "you need to be spending quality time with your children" was often the comment I heard. I remembered from my childhood the

time I spent hitchhiking with my Father and that my Father and I were probably closer to each other then, than at any other time in my life. I reasoned that my children would be better off if I simply shared my life with them and I hoped that I was right. Many of the other Artists were bringing their families to the shows and Valerie and Kimberlee soon made friends with these other "Art Show Brats" and looked forward to each show and the fun they would have with their friends. Splashing in Salado Creek or in the shallow bay waters at Rockport were two highlights of each summer. Valerie and Kimberlee tended to tell their friends at school about their weekend adventures and many of the other kids were jealous. Soon, we were loading up one or two of Valerie and Kimberlee's Austin friends to join them in their weekend fun. This went on until Valerie and Kimberlee became teenagers and wanted to have a social life. At that point Martha stayed home to supervise and I went on alone, except for a few shows like Rockport and Salado which were too much fun for the girls and the summer show at Memorial City Mall where Valerie and Kimberlee did their back to school clothes shopping. Valerie went on to doing her own Art and showing with me during the summer rather than getting a part time job. She made more money in a weekend than she would have in a month and had time to have a social life during the week. Looking back, I am delighted to hear from both Valerie and Kimberlee that those times, going to Art Shows are some of their fondest memories! ✚

HELP FROM THE HOMELESS

I was showing my work at the Old Pecan Street Festival in Downtown Austin and went to my trailer to fetch a framed print and as I came out in the open and looked at the sky, I was shocked to see a looming thunderhead with shades of green underneath. I ran back to my booth and started pulling the sides down

on my tent while I shouted to the other Artists within earshot to do the same. Within a couple minutes the storm hit with over fifty mile per hour winds and the roof on my tent went straight up in the air and the panels that held my art began to whip around and the whole booth collapsed onto the street with sounds of breaking glass. As if to ad

This Painting was the official Poster Art for Austin's 1982 Pecan Street Festival.

insult to injury, the rain came in blowing sheets, flying level to the ground and water was running ankle deep.

Back to the calm before the storm. This part of Austin has a large homeless population and there was this homeless man, going thru the trash barrels, picking out beer cans and drinking any remaining beer while babbling incoherently. When the wind hit and the Art began to fly this homeless man jumped up and started helping me get my Art into one of the stores nearby and after helping me, he went to the rescue of three other Artists. He was mentally sharp as a tack and fast on his feet and handled the Artwork like a professional!

Fortunately, none of my Paintings were damaged in spite of broken frames and shattered glass and had it not been for this homeless man, there would of certainly been lots of water damage. I pulled out a twenty dollar bill and handed it to him and the other Artists handed him money and we all thanked him with great enthusiasm. He looked at his new found fortune, stuffed it into his shirt and went back to babbling incoherently and wandered off down the street. It was almost unbelievable to watch him change back to his former self.

I have wondered ever since, if there is a cure for mental illness that can be gained by analyzing the changes in body chemistry that happen during emergencies. ✦

FREEWAY ART

I was showing my work at the Memorial City Mall, fall Art Show and had been getting my prints produced in Houston at the San Jacinto Graphic Center, so I arranged to have the print run scheduled for early in the morning on Friday so that I could get back to the mall early, so as to not miss very much of the open hours of the show. Jim Kirkpatrick, an Artist friend, was staying in the motor home and since I was heading out early, he suggested that I take his station wagon and let him sleep a little later,

since the mall didn't open until 10 am. I had taken the four Original Paintings out of the frames to save space, since I wasn't showing them in the show and had put them in a box that had contained glass for framing. I got to San Jacinto Graphic Center at 7:00 AM and they had two presses side by side with my prints being run simultaneously to speed things up. I took the Originals out and set them on easels beside the presses to compare with the prints for proofing.

The proofing went well and I was looking at being back at the Art Show by 11:00. I put the Paintings back in the glass storage box and was headed for the door, when "Charlie" my sales representative at San Jacinto Graphic Center, walked out with me and told me that he was retiring and wanted to tell me good bye. I stopped and put the box with the Paintings on the roof of Jim's car, since the car door was still locked and chatted with Charlie for a while. I then jumped in the car and headed back to the mall. I pulled up beside

the motor home to transfer the Paintings and was shocked when I opened the back of Jim's station wagon to find the Paintings missing. It hit me like a ton of bricks that I had left the paintings on the roof of the car back at San Jacinto Graphic Center! The Paintings had all been sold and I had borrowed them for the print run and I didn't have the money to give the owners a refund.

Where was I going to come up with over $20,000. I was sick to my stomach, but I jumped in the car and sped off in a frenzy, hoping for a miracle. San Jacinto Graphic Center was over ten miles from the mall and I was imagining the paintings being ground to bits by half a million cars.

As I got close to where I had entered the freeway, I saw the box leaning on the median on the other side of the freeway and it looked to be intact. I had to exit and turn around and get back on the freeway heading back toward the mall and was a nervous wreck thinking that someone would run over them before I could get there. Due to heavy traffic, it took what seemed like an eternity to get back around to where I could get to the box. I finally got back on the freeway and fought my way to the center lane.

The cars ahead of me were all swerving to the right and as I approached the box it was still leaning on the median and it still looked to be intact. The box was tilted toward the oncoming traffic and the big red letters "GLASS" were very visible, which probably explained why no one had run over it. I stopped right there, (fortunately traffic was moving slow) flung the door open, jumped out, grabbed the box, shoved it into the car and took off with a chorus of blowing horns behind me. Miraculously, all four of the Paintings were in perfect condition and I thanked God and my Guardian Angel for covering for my stupidity! The Texas Wild Bunch, an Artist group of which I am a member, had a tradition of presenting the "Buford Award" (a sculpture of a cowboy sinking into a cow patty) to the member that did the most stupid thing in a calendar year and I won the Buford Award without a challenger that was even close!

This is one of the four paintings that was in the box that ended up on the Houston Freeway in the above story!

SNOWBIRDS

(Written in 1985) On January second I looked out my studio window at the first of three snowstorms to fall on Austin this year. This pair of Cardinals have frequented our bird feeders for several years and were quite striking in contrast with the gray sky and bare branches of this tree in our backyard. Although I was working on another painting at the time, I immediately put it aside and started on this painting.

THE WORST ART SHOW I EVER HAD

The worst Art Show I ever had was in Brownwood, Texas and was called the Pecan Valley Art and Craft Fair. I made no sales and the only transaction that I made was an advance order for a Print that I was to ship several months later when the Print was to be published. I was to ship the print and the customer would send me a check when he received the Print. Well, I shipped the print and never got paid.

Three years later I received a call from the customer who was at the Austin Airport. (I was part of a group of Artists that had a display at the Airport) This man's name was Julian Trussell and he said "I'm out here at the Austin Airport, looking at your work and I believe I owe you some money!" I told him he did and he said, "I'm not a deadbeat, my wife ran me off right after I ordered your print and I forgot all about this until now." Then he asked me if I would take a credit card over the phone and when I said I would, he told me to add $50 to the total to make up for my troubles in collecting from him.

He apologized again and then asked me if I ever showed my work in the Bryan, College Station area. I told him that I hadn't and he asked me if I would consider showing my work in a Mall. I told him that I had shown my work at Houston's Memorial City Mall in their annual Art Fair and he said" The company I work for owns the Mall here in Bryan and I'll be glad to set you up in the Mall for free and we'll even do some advertising for you! I took him up on his offer and had a great show. Julian Trussell was very well connected in the community and he sent lots of his friends to the show and personally bought several more of my works. I showed at the Mall several more times over the next few years until a new Mall was built, which virtually put the older Mall out of business.

Julian changed jobs and moved to Mobile, Alabama, but before he did, he gave me some advice on how to show my work at the new Mall and other Malls. Julian introduced me to the right people at the new Post Oak Mall where I have continued to show my work and still sell work to many of Julian's friends.

I can't begin to count the amount of money I have made as a result of having the worst show of my career in Brownwood, Texas! ⬥

This is the Painting that Julian Trussell ordered a print of at the worst show of my career!

MY FRONT YARD Frequently my paintings result from my travels around the state, however I occasionally see things in my own yard that are equally interesting. Until we had our plumbing replaced, this dripping yard faucet provided a constant water source for many of our wild friends!

MEN ARE WIMP. AND CAN'T HANDLE PAIN!

I was about to leave for a show in Midland and was finishing my chores before leaving and the last thing I needed to do was feed my four horses a little sweet feed. I was standing beside my most gentle horse, putting out feed, when one of my other horses bit the horse that I was standing close to. She flinched and kicked at the biting horse, hitting my lower leg in the process.

I ran out of the way and pulled off my shoe and sock and examined my leg. I really hurt but I was able to rotate my ankle and determined that it probably was OK in spite of the pain. It's supposed to hurt when a horse kicks you, so I got into the motor home and headed for Midland. The pain had eased up some by the time I got to Midland but got a little worse during setup.

I stood up for the better part of four days and my leg seemed better (the swelling was almost gone). At the end of the show, I loaded up and headed back home for 2 days and then headed out for another show in Houston. I unloaded, set up and then stood on my feet for 4 more days and by the end of the show my leg had very little pain.

As I was loading up, I twisted my ankle and all of the pain came back and then some. By the time I got back to the ranch my leg was swollen so much that I had to remove my shoe. The next morning Martha looked at my leg and demanded that I go to the Doctor! I returned from the Doctor with my leg in a cast and sporting a pair of crutches. My fibula (small lower leg bone) was broken when the horse kicked me and had started to heal and I had re-broken it when I twisted my ankle loading up in Houston! Martha had always said that men couldn't handle pain, like a woman who had experienced child birth! She had to admit that maybe I was a little tougher than she thought! I had fun for a day tooling around on the crutches but woke up the next morning with every muscle in my upper body sore which made the pain from the broken leg seem trivial!

MORNING HUES I didn't have to go very far to find this barn, it's behind our house and three of the horses used to belong to us. The one that kicked me is on the left!

HOIGHTY TOIGHTY SHOW AT NEIMAN MARCUS

Neiman Marcus is known for very expensive merchandise and status items. Several years ago, they had a promotion to spotlight Texas Artisans and I was invited to show some of my work. The Houston Neiman Marcus is in the Galleria Mall in Houston and I was met on their loading dock by a young man who was in charge of their retail displays and told in great detail exactly how to hang my work. (like I had never hung a Painting before)

After micro managing every aspect of my showing, he told me that if I had a sale, I should get one of their sales people to handle it. My show was in the Couture Department and for those of you that are unrefined, that's where the rich lady sits on a plush couch, while Fashion Models parade in front of her wearing the latest exclusive fashions. Upon selecting her outfit the rich lady is measured and the outfit or gown is custom tailored for a perfect fit.

Some of these outfits will cost more than a luxury sedan and often are worn only one time!

All of the sales ladies seemed to have French or other European accents and acted like "they" were the rich ladies. Well, one of the husbands of one of the actual rich ladies wandered over to my Art work and after talking to him for a while, he decided to buy a painting. I tried to get the attention of one of the sales ladies but wasn't having much luck. (I guess they had no interest in mingling with a commoner like me) I finally stepped right in front of one of the sales ladies and said "I need you to handle a sale for me", to which she replied in her French accent "sooo sowwie messeur but I haav a custuumiir."

I had noticed several of these sales ladies coming and going thru a curtained passage way and thought maybe, the cash register might be hidden back there (you shouldn't have something as commercial and crass as a cash register in plain view in and area where your clothing costs more than a West Texas Ranch) I ventured thru the curtain and sure enough there was that evil cash register complete with an attendant who didn't speak French and was more than glad to run my customer's credit card. There was a large rack of clothing beside the register and as I was about to go back into the store, two of the sales ladies came in and not seeing me behind the rack of clothes, dropped their French accents and started talking Texan. The last lady that had brushed me off, said to the other lady in a thick East Texas Drawl "aat Biitch is driivin me nuts." Suddenly, she noticed me and gave out with a gasp and said "don't tell my customer what I just said". I said, "don't worry" and left to give my customer his Painting.

I guess that the word got out that I knew their secret because the sales ladies got much friendlier with me after that and when things slowed down close to closing time the sales lady that I caught trash talking came over and looked at my work and related to me that she had always aspired to be an actress but had fallen in love and settled down in Houston with her husband and said "This is as close as I get, to being an actress" ⬥

LIGHTNING BEARD

I was showing my work at the Kaleidoscope Art Fair in Beaumont and on Saturday evening, about an hour before closing time, a big thunderstorm rolled in and although our Art was under a big tent the torrential rain came down with so much intensity that within minutes the ground inside the tent was totally covered with a couple inches of water.

The Booth next to mine was Photography and the next booth down the line was a Pottery booth. I happened to be looking in the direction of the two adjoining booths and noticed the Photographer's wife having a conversation with the heavily bearded Potter in the next booth, while both stood in ankle deep water. What happened next was one of the strangest sights I have ever seen. The Potter had one hand on a metal tent pole when lightning struck nearby and a bolt of lightning came out of the tip of the Potter's beard and struck the Photographer's wife in the chest, knocking her to the ground. Apparently the lightning wasn't a full charge, because the Photographer's wife got right up and although being pretty wet, seemed to be just fine.

Neither she nor the Potter seemed to be aware that they had been struck by lightning until a few of us that witnessed the bizarre incident told them about it. The Potter's beard was a little singed but other than that there were no adverse effects. ⬥

BIKIN' THRU BEAUMONT This theater is directly across the street from the Art Museum of Southeast Texas that hosted the Kaleidoscope Art Fair! The Jefferson Theater, built in 1927, is in Downtown Beaumont, Texas and "Baby The Rain Must Fall" was filmed in Southeast Texas in 1964. I'm told that Country Singer George Jones ushered there, also that the World Premier's of "It's a Wonderful Life" and "Babe" were held there and that Steve McQueen lived in Beaumont for a short time. Any resemblance to Steve on the motorcycle is purely intentional!

GUESS WHO'S COMING TO DINNER!

As I mentioned earlier, I am a member of a group of Artists called the "Texas Wild Bunch".

Well, the Wild Bunch was having a show at Memorial Mall in Houston and the founder of our group, Harley Murray, had been teaching a workshop prior to the show with the Katy Art League which was made up of primarily "Rich Ladies" who dabbled in Art. Well the ladies from the Katy Art League came out to our show and invited us all to have supper on Saturday evening after the show closed. We all showed up at the hostesse's house and were gabbing with the Art League Ladies when one of our Wild Bunch Members, Burl Washington rang the doorbell. Burl, who happens to have a little darker skin than the rest of us is a great Artist and a really great guy. Burl has a tremendous sense of humor and delights in racial humor. If all Black folks were like Burl there would be no racial problems in our society. Well, it quickly became obvious that these Art League Ladies had never socialized with a Black person because they were all paying so much attention to Burl that it was making him uncomfortable (which is really hard to do) Harley Murray, who had a reputation for being a Joker, noticed all the attention being payed to Burl and at the first opportunity, sat down by Burl and started talking to him. I noticed Burl and Harley snickering and grinning and figured that they were cooking something up.

A little later when the food was ready and we were all about to sit down and eat, Harley said in a rather loud voice "Burl, they have your food in the Back Room!" A shock wave went thru the Art League Ladies and they were gasping for breath and looking totally bewildered and having trouble talking. Burl was silent until the gasping stopped and when attention returned to him he said with a big grin "you mean, dey got Watermelon back dere?" All of us Wild Bunch Artists roared with laughter and Harley and Burl slapped hands and gave each other a bear hug. After that, the Katy Art League Ladies were a lot more relaxed and the evening went really well. I like to think that the next time these ladies socialized with a Black person that they would just treat them like any other friend! ⬦

PLAYING THE LOWBALL

I was showing my work at the Salado Art Fair and my booth was next to an Artist friend of mine named Don Easterwood. Don had to take a nature break and asked me to watch his booth. When Don came back he had a big grin on his face and told me about a prank he wanted to play on a local Doctor, who I will call "Dr. Lowball".

This Doctor was particularly obnoxious and would always make ridiculously low offers to Artists, trying to buy the work as cheaply as possible. No Artist that I know of appreciates this type of bargaining. We put a lot of ourselves into our work and having somebody ask us to cut our prices is insulting and only those Artists who are desperate will cut their prices. So, as you can

I was honored to have this work published as the Poster for the 2006 Salado Art Fair. When I was asked to do a Painting for the Poster I didn't think I had enough time to produce a new Painting so I got on my computer and took pieces from several of my Paintings and assembled them into a new work in a program called Photoshop. Although the components of this picture are all my work, there is no original!

probably guess, Dr. Lowball hadn't collected any work from Don or me.

There was an Artist I'll call "Desperate Dan" who really needed money to survive and had buried his pride in order to survive and was taking any offer he could to generate whatever money he could.

Don outlined the prank. He had seen Dr. Lowball carrying a large snow scene out of Desperate Dan's booth and since he would have to pass our booths on his way to the exit, Don waited until Dr. Lowball was within earshot and pretending not to notice Dr. Lowball, turned his back and faced me and said in a rather loud voice "Hey, Boutwell, old Desperate Dan is one happy boy right now." I said "why's that", Don said, "you know that big old snow scene he's been carrying around for years? well, he finally unloaded that dog!" ("dog" is a term that Artist's apply to a Painting that they think will never sell)

Dr. Lowball had a worried look on his face and slouched away, probably wondering who took advantage of who! I guess he found out how it feels loose a little pride! ✦

BRIDGE UNDER TROUBLED WATERS

My first Art Show outside of Austin was the Salado Art Fair on the first weekend of August in 1969. The show was held on the Village Green on both sides of Salado Creek where a small dam creates a delightful pond. Artists were not assigned booth space and the entrance was roped off and all of the Artists waited by the entrance until the Fair Officials dropped the rope and then we all scrambled to claim our spots. Total pandemonium broke out and even one fist fight over disputed territory. I stood there in disbelief and waited until things settled down to select my spot as I only had about a dozen works and some wire floral easels that I had gotten free from a cemetery. I found a small spot on the banks of Salado Creek and proceeded to set up my work which took all of ten minutes (these days it takes around 6 hours). The show opened and I was surprised to win third place in Watercolor! The Army Corps of Engineers had set up a temporary

Pontoon Bridge across the pond to allow people to access both sides of the show and people seemed to enjoy crossing on that temporary bridge. As the day wore on the crowd increased and the Pontoon Bridge became busier to the point that it's load capacity was overwhelmed and it slowly started sinking into the pond. People screamed in panic in what looked to be a scene out of a Godzilla Movie, until they realized that the pond wasn't very deep and they were only knee deep in the water when the bridge hit the bottom of the pond. Everyone regained their dignity and proceeded to leave the bridge until it resurfaced as it's load lessened. ✦

PRESIDENTIAL COLLECTION (ALMOST)

In May of 1972, I was showing my Art at the Texas State Arts and Craft Fair in Kerrville and we were told that President Lyndon B. Johnson's wife Lady Bird would be previewing the show. All of the Artists were told to open their booths early for the First Lady. The fair management came thru the show and roped off the booths and we Artists were told to exit our booths and stand outside the tents and roped off area. Lady Bird came down the walkway at a rather fast pace, barely glancing into the booths and when she got to my booth the Original of this Pen and Ink Drawing caught her attention and she stopped and went into my booth and knelt down to have a better look. She got up, came out of the booth, made eye contact with me and said, " that is very nice" (referring to the Train Drawing). She then walked away at her former brisk pace, barely looking at the other booths. A Secret Service Agent approached me almost before Lady Bird was out of sight and told me that Lady Bird would like to have the Train Drawing for her collection. I was thinking to myself that this was my lucky day because I would now be able to brag about my work being in a President's collection. I asked the Secret Service Agent how payment was to be arranged and he told me that I was expected to donate the Drawing. I had spent close to 75 hours on the Drawing and was only asking $75 for it and the idea of giving it away kind of rubbed me the wrong way and I told him that the Johnson's were perfectly capable of paying $75 dollars and that I would not donate the Drawing. The Secret service Agent told me that I was missing out on a big opportunity! I don't know for

sure if Lady Bird really wanted the Drawing or if she really expected me to give it to her, my suspicion is that the Secret Service Agent was trying to win favor with Lady Bird.

Minutes after this incident, in the next tent, a more opportunistic Artist was poised with a Painting in hand, a Photographer standing by and as Lady Bird approached, he thrust the Painting over the ropes into her hands and turned and smiled while the Photographer shot pictures which were published the next day in the Kerrville Newspaper!

I know it's the way of the world but (since becoming a Christian) I have always believed that any honors or publicity that come my way should be legitimate!

Nadija Fuller worked for me as a picture framer in the 1990's and she sent a framed print of Memory Lane to Bill Clinton. Bill responded with a handwritten thank you letter so I guess I'm in a Presidential Collection after all! 🖐

YOU'RE OUTTA HERE, WELL, MAYBE

The Texas Wild Bunch had had several shows at Hulen Mall in Fort Worth and we had just set up there again and were open for a couple of hours when we were confronted by a young lady who was from the mall office and asked why we were set up in the mall. Randy Souders, the Artist who had handled the contact with the mall, lived in Fort Worth and had gone home to clean up. The girl from the mall demanded to see our contract and if we couldn't produce it, she was going to evict us from the mall immediately.

We told her that Randy had handled the arrangements with the mall manager and that he was due to return shortly. The young lady said that the mall manager was out of town on vacation and that there wasn't any way he could be reached

SHOWERS OF SUNSHINE I was working on this Painting at the Hulen Mall show in the story above! This title resulted from my annual contest to name one of my prints. Sunrays breaking through dark clouds always remind me that no matter how gloomy things may appear, there is always hope and of how lucky we all are to be alive and able to enjoy the beauty of this world!

and she was in charge and we had better produce a contract! This young lady had recently been transferred to Fort Worth by the mall's parent corporation and had no idea how this mall manager operated. Randy showed up and we told him of our peril and he said that there was no contract, that the mall manager had always had a verbal agreement with him.

Our hopes were sinking fast when Randy had a brainstorm and a strategy was formed in his mind!

To give some background on Randy, Randy Souders was injured in a swimming accident in High School and he has been confined to a wheel chair since that time. His positive attitude about life and his success as an Artist over incredible odds are an inspiration to everyone who knows him!

Randy told us to stall her for a while, so he could go back home to get some proof that we were supposed to be in the mall.

Randy has always said his wheelchair is a great gimmick and

that the sympathy factor is a great negotiating tool. Randy returned to the mall and went into the office, armed with a cassette from his answering machine, wheeled up to the young lady's desk and told her that the cassette was from his answering machine and that the mall manager had left a message about the Wild Bunch having our show and offered to play the tape for her. The young lady looked a little shaken and said it wouldn't be necessary and apologized for her harshness and allowed our show to proceed. Randy came out of the mall office with a big grin on his face and told us that the mall manager had indeed left a message on his answering machine but that the tape had been erased and had nothing on it! He then said "no one want's to be mean to a guy in a wheelchair, so I thought I had a pretty good chance with my little bluff." The young lady came out of her office several times during our show and made a point of being incredibly nice to us and complimented all of us on our work.

I guess she was trying to butter us up so that we wouldn't report her actions to the mall manager when he returned from vacation! ⬥

LOST IN THE OZONE

Back in the seventies I had been trying to promote my work on a national level and was doing shows all over the country. I had designed and built a folding display that was light and compact, that I could strap together and ship by air for a reasonable amount.

I had an employee named Ronnie Bittick who enjoyed doing shows and he had done several shows for me. Ronnie was scheduled to show my work at a convention in Los Angeles, California and I had scheduled The Coconut Grove Art Festival in Miami Florida, two days after Ronnie's show.

Ronnie was to pack up his Los Angeles Show and ship the Art and the folding display to Miami for me to pick up at the air freight office in Miami when I arrived there. I packed up some extra Artwork and left Austin and flew into Miami and rented a van at the airport. I drove over to the air freight office at the Miami airport to pick up my Art and display and to my surprise, the Art was there but the display wasn't. The agent at the air freight office said that there were three more flights coming in that night and that maybe my display would arrive on one of those flights. By midnight my display was nowhere to be seen and I had gotten to know the air freight agent pretty well by that time.

I noticed that each time a plane unloaded that wooden freight palettes would be stacked up in a corner of the freight warehouse, so I asked the freight agent if I could borrow several of the freight palettes to build a makeshift display booth. The agent said he could also loan me a hammer and a sack of nails, so I loaded up several of the freight palettes and headed down to the Coconut Grove.

As I left the airport, I got pulled over by a policeman and was ticketed for an expired inspection sticker on the rental van. I had assumed that I could find a motel room close to the show but found that there wasn't a room to be had anywhere in the area. I was exhausted and it was about 2:00 a.m., so I pulled into a parking lot close to the show and slept in the van. I got up and checked in at the show set up booth and went to my booth area and proceeded to nail the freight palettes together into a makeshift booth. When I finished constructing the booth I was amazed at how good it looked. I used some of the nails to hang my work and was finishing up when an Artist I knew named Andy Chapman from Mobile, Alabama came by and asked me what happened to my regular set up. I related my story to Andy and asked him if he knew of any motel rooms in the area. Andy said he had his motor home parked a couple blocks away and that I could sleep on the couch in the motor home.

The show opened and I sold enough work to come away with a good profit and got lots of compliments from other Artists on my booth made from freight palettes. Back in those days none of us Artists had tents or canopies, we just carried rolls of plastic that we would throw over our work if it started to rain and fortunately I had included a roll of plastic with my work because we had a Saturday afternoon thunderstorm. I packed up the rental van on Sunday afternoon and went back to the air freight office and returned the freight palettes and hammer and checked in the boxes with my Artwork in them for shipment back to Austin. My display panels had still not arrived and the freight agent took down my address to send them to Austin when they arrived.

To this day my display panels have never been found and I returned to the Coconut Grove Art Show a couple more times, but I drove down to Miami in my motor home. 🪓

ANOTHER GREAT DAY This was inspired in the Big Thicket at sunrise at Livingston, Texas. I was going thru the drive thru line at McDonalds to get some breakfast and saw this scene!

STEPPING OFF THE COWBOY ELEVATOR

In the 1980's Western Art was where the money was and I found myself being swept up in the trend. I had been to several ranches to take photographs and had some good material to work from. I was advertising my work in Southwest Art Magazine and getting invited to show my work in some of the top Western Art shows and it looked like I was on my way to the top.

I was showing my work in Cody, Wyoming at the Buffalo Bill Memorial Art Show and not only sold well but won first place in Watercolor. The competition at this show was particularly intense as most of the Artists in the show were nationally known! The judge was Nick Eggenhoffer, an icon in the Western Art world and by the end of this show I was feeling pretty important.

The Buffalo Bill Museum at the time housed the largest collection of Charles Russell works in the world as well as a hefty collection of Frederick Remmington's work. For those of you not aware of the history of Western Art, Remmington and Russell were the first and foremost Artists of their era and the founders of Western Art! So, after the show, we went to the museum to view the works of Western Art's "God Fathers" and I was in for one of the biggest surprises of my Art career.

The Charles Russell works were arranged more or less in the order that they were created and the early work was terrible, I wouldn't have signed it, it was so bad, but his work got steadily better until it became masterful. I realized that the journalists that had sung his praises had led me to believe that Charles Russell was born, a Master. It was obvious that he also had to learn and gradually improve just like the rest of us mortals and that maybe I had the potential to be as good an Artist someday. Then it hit me like a ton of bricks, I was viewing Charles Russell's life thru his work, he was there in the old west and he portrayed the life he was living.

I asked myself, "why am I trying to paint Charles Russell's life? I didn't live in the old west, I should be painting my own life!" All the way, driving back to Texas I pondered the question of who I was and what my life was about until I realized that "I was a Redneck Kid that grew up in Texas in the 1950's!"

This was an abrupt turning point in my career and I decided to restrict my showing and painting to Texas and started reflecting on my own experiences. I was aware that much of the culture of the fifties was rapidly vanishing. Neon signs were being replaced by backlit plastic, businesses that reflected the personality of the owners were being replaced by ones that all looked alike. I felt that it would all soon be lost. I had painted old rusty cars in the past but now I was more interested in making them look new.

I embarked on a quest to chronicle this fading era that I had lived thru, with the Gas Stations, Drive Inns, Motels and the other Icons of the disappearing culture. Maybe, I had the potential to be in my own era, what Charles Russell was in his! 🇹🇽

HAVE I STAYED TOO LONG AT THE FAIR?

Having shown my work at various Art & Craft Fairs for 42 years, I'm often asked how and why, at my age, (68 at the time of this writing) I can keep going down the road at such an intense pace. I participated in my first Art in the park show when I was 26 and enjoyed it more than dealing with Art galleries.

In the 1960's there was a lot of interest in Art and most towns had an Art group that sponsored an annual Art show in a park, on a courthouse square or at a civic center. There was a feeling of comradery among the Artists and I enjoyed meeting people and selling my work without having to satisfy some "expert," before the public viewed my Art.

It was a time of change in the Art world and it was exciting to be a part of this new Art Movement. As I continued to show my work and the years flew by, I noticed that my energy level was much higher when I was working a show and that I seemed to have a mental image of my self as being a young man full of energy and enthusiasm.

When I am off the road for a month each December, I start to wonder if I am still up to working so hard, "setting up my display generally takes at least six hours and tearing down my display takes between four and five hours. "

Loading up for the first show of the new year is a tiring, grueling experience. Somehow, as I head down the road and as each mile flashes by, my energy level starts to rise and I seem to forget my age and become 26 years old again!

I carry my painting gear in my motor home and often sit and paint until midnight, after my show has closed for the day and I am constantly stopping to photograph interesting things, as I travel to and from my shows.

Before I started working shows, I was very introverted and lacked social confidence (I was the typical wallflower at any social event). Showing my work seemed to draw me out of my shell and after several shows, with a parade of people complementing me and buying my work, my confidence rose and I became comfortable being the center of attention.

So, I have the choice of either being an old introverted geezer or being a 26 year old, confident, energetic, outgoing young dude (at least in my mind). Which choice would you make?

CLEAN UP CREW After we fed our horses a bucket of oats, A covey of Bobwhite Quail would come and pick up any leftovers.

121

MODERN ARTIST EXTRAORDINAIRE

While I was working at one of my Commercial Art jobs, one of my co-workers who had a college Art degree was trying to break into the modern Art world.

There was one modern Art gallery in Austin at the time and there was one evening each month, that the gallery held a "Submission Night." Aspiring modern Artists would come and bring their portfolios with hopes of showing in the gallery.

My co-worker would do new work each month and take it to the gallery only to be rejected each time. My co-worker and I got along well as long as we didn't discuss Art because he felt that modern Art was far superior to my "naive realism" and that since I didn't have an Art degree, I didn't have the intellectual capacity to appreciate "True Art". In those days there was a commercial Art medium called Flourographic, that was used to produce inexpensive color illustrations that involved painting three separate transparent Mylar overlays with yellow, red and blue in sequence over a black and white drawing, so that when they were viewed one on top of the other you could see how the illustration would look when printed in color.

One day while I was working on an Illustration, I had a stack of Mylar sheets on a table next to my desk and had the open bottles of Flourographic medium on my desk.

The phone rang and as I turned to answer, I accidentally knocked two of the bottles off the desk and they fell onto the table below and spilled onto the Mylar. The pure colors ran together and produced a bright colorful flow of intermingling color and I had one of my wild ideas and thought to myself, "Submission Night".

On Saturday I went to the Art supply store and bought a package of Mylar and several bottles of the Flourographic medium. I went home and spread the Mylar out on the floor of my home studio and proceeded to spill and squirt the colors onto the Mylar. Daughters, Valerie and Kimberlee (ages 4 and 7) helped, We tilted some of the Mylar Sheets to make the colors flow and spattered denatured alcohol on others with a toothbrush, making what looked like swimming Amoeba in the flowing colors.

I cropped the painted Mylar sheets into interesting shapes, mounted them on white matt board, that I had signed and then cut white matts to fit each painting. I ended up with about twenty finished pieces and proceeded to go to the modern Art gallery on "Submission Night."

The trend in Modern Art at the time was toward dark colors and shades of gray and brown and my colors were bright and intense. The owner of the modern Art gallery was "Blown Away" with my work and accepted them with great enthusiasm and extolled the virtues of my work in big words that I didn't even understand.

In less than two weeks all of my works had sold and I was asked to bring more. I was proclaimed to be the gallery's "Star Artist". After we produced a couple more batches of these abstract paintings which sold almost as quickly, I was feeling guilty for profiting from what I considered to be a hoax.

The Art gallery owner told me that she had a colleague that owned a gallery in New York City and that they wanted to show my work. I might have been a fool to say no, but I had spent my life learning to draw and paint realistic work and I didn't want to throw that away and become famous for something I had no respect for. I told the gallery owner that I was a realist and that I had done the abstract work to prove a point to a co-worker and that I would not be producing any more modern Art. I then found out how well rounded this refined, intellectual woman was because in addition to knowing words that I didn't understand, she also knew lots of common street expletives that she directed at me with great vigor!

Thus ended my modern Art career and my co-worker never mentioned my lack of intellect again!

I never took any photographs of my modern art paintings that I refer to in the story above, so I decided to include a Bluebonnet Painting on the same page as the modern art story. For those of you that have not been around the Texas modern art crowd, a Bluebonnet Painting is just about the antithesis of modern art and probably the one thing most reviled by those folks!

FIELD OF GLORY This title is the result of my annual contest to name one of my Paintings. The Church is west of our ranch between Norse and Cranfill's Gap and is known in the area as the Rock Church. I was standing by a single Oak Tree when I took my reference photographs but decided when I was painting the picture to add some more trees to balance the picture!

OVERNIGHT HORSE EXPERT

While I was living in Austin, I was privileged to be invited to come out and take photographs on the Anchor X ranch in Lampassas which was managed by Morris Vann who owned the adjacent ranch. I took hundreds of photographs and actually got in the saddle and helped work cattle. (there will be a detailed story of this event later in the book) The Anchor X owners Gardner and Mary Ann Parker and manager, Morris Vann were quite pleased with the paintings that I produced.

I later, made prints of some of the paintings from the Anchor X and from paintings I had done from the Stamford Cowboy Reunion. I took the prints to my Art Shows and was forever being criticized by "self proclaimed horse experts" who typically told me that the "conformation" of my horses was wrong. I would then ask my critic to explain what was wrong with the "conformation" of my horses and the typical answer would be "you just have to live it to understand"

I started paying attention to the conversations prior to being criticized and realized, that these "experts" usually asked me where I lived and were assuming that since I was a "city slicker" from Austin that they could "mouth off," assuming I was ignorant about horses.

Well, after we bought the ranch and I traded Art for horses and cattle, I started noticing that after I told one of these "horse expert types" that I lived on a ranch, the comment typically would be "its obvious that you know your horses, your conformation is perfect!"

Funny thing was, that the prints that these "experts" were complimenting me on, were the same prints that I got criticized on before we moved to the ranch!

IN THE NICK OF TIME Although the scene is near Hillsboro, this painting was inspired by a thunderstorm at Midland. I had set my work up at an outdoor show at the Art Museum of the Southwest and had gone to the Petroleum Museum. I looked outside and saw a big storm rolling in and raced back to the show to cover my work!

SECONDS TO SPARE I was traveling between Stamford and Albany, Texas when I saw this couple, hurriedly gathering the wash as a Thunderhead loomed over them. Their house was actually a mobile home but the impending storm and their situation kicked my creativity into high gear, I did a little substituting and this Painting was the result! I was gassing up in Cisco on my way to the Cowboy Reunion at Stamford, when this 1958 Chevy pulled up at the next pump and I jumped into the motor home, grabbed my camera and shot a bunch of pictures. Since I photographed the 1958 Chevy on the same trip as the inspiration for the Painting above, it just seemed natural to include it in the Painting!

A BUNCH OF STORIES AND PAINTINGS THAT HAVE NOTHING TO DO WITH EACH OTHER!

PACK RAT FINDS JUSTIFICATION

I can't help it, I'm a Pack Rat!, no matter how hard I try to throw stuff away, I always seem to come up with some reason to keep things.

You never know when you are going to need stuff you thought you never would need, but if you don't keep it, someday you will need it and you will have to go and buy another and a fella could go broke that way!

Well after stuff piles up and no one can even get into the room, Martha finally threatens to hurt me and I grudgingly go thru and verbally defend each item as she points menacingly to the Trash Can.

The one safe area for all my junk is my studio, where I am the absolute monarch because I can claim it to be reference material!

When we were moving to the ranch, I had rented a box van and made several trips to the ranch, with full loads and was closing in on the last load, which was all the stuff in my studio. I was really tired, when I found two large cardboard boxes, under one of my tables, that were taped shut and had been there for more than ten years. For that matter, they had been moved there from our previous house and hadn't been opened in all of those years.

The boxes were heavy and when I got them down the stairs and out to where I was loading the truck, it occurred to me, that I would either have to make another trip to the ranch, or I could throw some of my junk in the trash and be done with the move.

Well I reasoned that whatever was in those two boxes hadn't been needed in over ten years and that if I opened them, I would come up with some reason to keep some of the contents and I really didn't have time for that, as it was getting late and I needed to get on the road. I put them out with the trash and headed for the ranch!

When I got to the ranch, I told Martha, that I had thrown away some things and she was so proud of me and said, "see that didn't hurt all that bad, maybe there's hope that you can change your ways!"

Well, after eight years passed, our first Grandson, Josh was born and when he was about one and a half years old, Martha decided to read him a bedtime story and asked me, "where did you put all of the story books that we read to Valerie and Kimberlee when they were little?"

I had this sinking feeling and after much searching it became obvious that I had thrown them away in those two taped up heavy boxes!

Since that day, Martha had been in charge of anything that gets thrown away! ✦

BOY, "DID YOU COPY THAT PICTURE OFF THE TV?"

I found this painted windmill up in the Texas panhandle near the town of Post. Although the fan looked like the one in this painting, the tail was painted with red, white and blue stripes. The minute I saw this windmill I said to myself "these folks almost got this right, the tail of this windmill should have a Texas flag on it"

So, since I was planning a "Texas windmill calendar", I proceeded to put the Texas flag on the windmill in my painting.

In late 1992, after the windmill calendar was published and we had mailed the calendars to everyone that had ordered them, I got a call from one of my customers named Jerry Lackey from San Angelo, Texas. Jerry told me that he was the star of a statewide television show called the "Texas Farm and Ranch Report"

that aired on Sundays. Jerry asked me if he could use my Texas flag windmill painting as a backdrop for his television show. He said that this painting was perfect for the Texas Farm and Ranch Report and I agreed to let him use the painting on his show.

Not long after the Texas flag windmill aired on Jerry's show,

rancher's started painting Texas flags on their windmills and small scale models were being offered for sale all over Texas. As far as I know, I was the first to put a Texas flag on a windmill.

I'm still having people come up to me at my Art shows and ask me "did you copy that picture off that TV show?"

PRIDE OF TEXAS I found this Windmill when I was wandering aimlessly in the Texas Panhandle near Post. It had Red, White and Blue Bars on the tail but I thought it needed to have a Texas Flag! The Print of this is the most popular thing I have ever done!

A PRANK, GONE GOOD

HOW I GOT THE OFFICIAL TEXAS STATE ARTIST TITLE.

Every year since the 1970's, the Texas State Legislature has chosen a State Artist, a Poet Laureate, a State Musician and a State Sculptor.

When I became aware of the title, I enquired with the information center at the State Capitol and was told that there was a committee consisting of three State Representatives and three State Senators who made the decision and to be considered for the title, an Artist had to be recommended by one of those six politicians. I found out that each of these politicians recommended an Artist from their respective district and that the only chance I had was to have my representative get appointed to the committee. I've never been good at politics so I abandoned the quest.

After we moved to the ranch we learned that Elizabeth Torrence, the Granddaughter of the original owner of our house lived in Clifton and we contacted her. Elizabeth came out to the ranch for the first time since her family sold the ranch and was quite emotional as she related her experiences of growing up in our house. Over the next few years we became good friends with Elizabeth and she became like part of our family.

Elizabeth was very active in local

SATURDAY MATINEE, When I was 13, in 1956, we rode the bus to downtown Austin every Saturday to see the Matinee at the Paramount Theater. The marquee has been removed from the Paramount in Austin but I found Abilene's Paramount theater and used it in this Painting. The other buildings are in Cuero, Shiner and Hico!

politics and hosted receptions for aspiring politicians. Elizabeth was an important worker in the campaign of our new State Representative and asked him to nominate me for the State Artist Title. He asked to be appointed to the State Artist Committee and was selected. I was nominated and went to the Capitol with the other five nominated Artists to show my work to the committee. I was not selected for the title but was nominated again the following year and went back for a second try.

By that time, I had figured out that the committee member with the most power and influence was probably making the decision and the rest of us nominees were only there so lend legitimacy to his selection. It occurred to me, that my state representative was a first term representative with no political clout and that, the "Big Dog" was making the decision. Well, my representative didn't run for a second term, so that was the end of my being nominated. I had struck out with the "Good Ol Boy Network"!

I forgot about the state Artist title for twelve years and had been told by a couple of other Artists that the State had discontinued the title.

One day, as I was sitting at my computer, writing my quarterly online newsletter, an Email came in from one of my customers, with a notice about the Official Texas State Artist title, which had been revived for the previous five years. The title was now being handled by the Texas Commission for the Arts and they were taking nominations from the public. The nominations were to be screened and finalists would be forwarded to the Legislature for a final vote!

I logged on to the Commission for

CRUISIN THE DIXIE QUEEN, This Drive In was in Jewett, Texas and was closed down when I photographed it in 1981. It reminded me of my teenage years and the nights we spent cruising from one end of Austin to the other, with no particular goal except to look cool and see who else was cruisin'. Wow ya'll, was that Elvis in that Merc?

the Arts website and found that all of the Artists, who had been given the title since it was reinstated, were academics (college Art professors) and did modern Art. I guessed that the Commission for the Arts had notified college Art departments and Art organizations about the title and that they were probably the only ones aware of the title.

Well, since I have no valid Art credentials, ie: Art degree, I figured my chances with the academics were probably less than I had had with the "good old boy network".

All of a sudden I had this fiendish idea! I was about to send an online newsletter to over eight thousand people, so I cut and pasted the information from the Texas Commission for the Arts into my newsletter and sent it out to all eight thousand people. My intent was to "rattle a few cages" as I figured that the Commission for the Arts was probably inhabited by academics.

Six months went by and one day I got a letter from the Commission for the Arts, stating that I had been nominated for the title of Texas State Artist and that I had about a week to submit samples of my work.

I figured that I had irritated them, but I probably had too many nominations to be ignored and that they would grudgingly take a look at my work. I reasoned that the decision makers were more than likely academics and that if I

GOOD OL' NIGHTS, The Chief Drive-In was in Austin, Texas on North Lamar Boulevard and Martha and I dated there when we were teenagers. I tried to include every car made in the fifties in this painting as well as some older ones, but I'm sure I missed one or two. Bet you never saw this movie!

130

submitted bluebonnets or western stuff, I would have a snowball's chance in hell of getting the title, so I sent in samples of my old car stuff, figuring that it was different enough that it might stand a chance. A year went by and I figured that they weren't notifying the losers, so I all but forgot about my little "E-Prank".

In June of 2005, "out of the blue" I got a phone call from the Director of the Commission for the Arts, telling me that I had been selected as the Official Texas State Artist for the year 2006! The Waco newspaper did an interview with me and also with the Director of the Commission for the Arts and found that I had received more nominations than any Artist in the history of the title and that based on that, they had submitted me as one of the finalists to the legislature for their vote. The newspaper reporter was told that I was selected almost unanimously. I guess the old cars and scenes of the fifties hit most of the Legislators in a soft spot and more than likely the other finalists were modernists, that the average

redneck didn't relate to.

The nomination process included the opportunity for those doing the nominating to also nominate candidates for the Poet Laureate, the State Musician and the State Sculptor. I suspect that my customers had some influence on those titles as well, since the previous honorees for Poet Laureate and State Musician had all also been academics. The Poet Laureate for 2006 was Red Steagall, cowboy poet and western entertainer (first

rhyming poet to get the title!), the State Musician was Billy Joe Shaver, country singer, songwriter and I guess my customers weren't familiar with any sculptors because the State Sculptor was a modernist.

By the way, anyone that nominates an Artist gets contacted in following years and is given the opportunity to nominate again, and as a probable result of all of my customers being on this list, all of the Official Texas State Artists since 2006 have been traditional Artists! **Rednecks Rule!**

AT THE CROSSROADS, If you travel down enough country roads you will find one of these treasures. Time seems to stand still and the main event in the world is either Moon or 42. "You can get the goods you really need here but you'll have to go down the road to get the stuff you just want."

FOLLOWING A HUNCH!

Martha and I go walking on the ranch in the morning and on this particular day, as we got down to the west fence line near Neil's Creek, Martha said that she wanted to walk the north fence line on the way back to the house. This section of fence is along some of the roughest terrain on the ranch and I tried to discourage her because I thought she might slip and fall and hurt herself if she made the walk, but she insisted and said, she just had a "feeling".

The roughest part of this stretch of fence is an area where erosion continues to carve out a small gorge under the fence. It has been necessary to string more and more barbed wire along the bottom of the fence as the gorge gets deeper. As a result this area of fence looks like a big twenty foot high net!

Well, as we approached the afore mentioned net area of the fence, there was this huge Great Horned Owl tangled up in the fence.

Martha approached the Owl,

HACKBERRY SAGE We rescued this Great Horned Owl from a tangle of barbed wire and I took some pictures. I placed him in an old dead Hackberry Tree and since Owls are a symbol of wisdom, I thought this title was appropriate!

talking to it in a soft voice and told me to find a good stick. I searched the debris that had accumulated at the bottom of the fence and found a stout tree branch that was about two inches in diameter and a couple of feet long.

An Owl is a vicious predator that is nothing to mess with, because, in addition to it's razor sharp beak, it has tremendous strength in it's feet. It kills it's prey by grabbing the animal with it's feet and literally crushing it, with its vise like grip. An Owl can break a human's arm in a matter of seconds by simply clamping down with it's feet!

Martha took the stick that I found and held it close to the Owl and told him to get on the stick. The Owl reached out and grabbed the stick as Martha was moving it under him. I took hold of the stick and lifted the Owl up and Martha got hold of his impaled wing and pulled it off of the barbed wire and the Owl settled down on the stick and we carried it back to the house, which was about a half mile away.

Martha has always had a talent of communicating with animals and the Owl seemed to be calmed by her talking softly to it. When we got back to the house we put the Owl in our greenhouse and went into the house to see what kind of meat we had in the refrigerator and to try and find someone with a Federal Raptor Permit (it is illegal to possess a bird of prey without a Federal Permit unless you are an American Indian)

We contacted the Wildlife Rescue group in Austin and were given the name and phone number of a man in Whitney, which is about twenty five miles away.

It took a couple of days to make contact with the permit holder in Whitney and the Owl seemed to adjust, just fine to the greenhouse and had a good appetite.

Meanwhile, the Artist in me couldn't resist taking lots of photographs of this beautiful Owl. When we finally made contact with the permit holder, we put the Owl in a carrying cage and delivered him to the permit holder who took charge of the rehabilitation. 🪵

ROYAL REST STOP, Every fall and spring, we are privileged to be visited my the migrating Monarch Butterflies as they pass thru our area. This is from the fall migration where they seemed to have replaced the fallen leaves

BUTTING HEADS WITH BUREAUCRATS

I've always tried to do things right in my business and as a result, had gotten professional help in the area of taxes and regulations necessary to set up a business. I thought that the reason that the big time accounting firms were so big was because they knew what they were doing and they must be good at what they do. Boy was I in for a surprise!

Back in about 1989, we hired a young lady to do secretarial work and told her that our policy was a thirty day trial and that at the end of thirty days she would either get a raise or be terminated depending on her performance. Well, she deliberately did everything possible to get fired and within an hour of being let go, she had filed for unemployment. (she had been coached in ways to get any and all possible government benefits)

The Texas Employment Commission contacted us about the filing and we protested by phone. In the process of our telephone hearing with the Employment Commission, I was asked for my Employer Identification Number, which I promptly gave them, only to be told that the number I gave them was a Federal Number and that they needed my State ID Number.

I told them that I would have to ask my big time accounting firm for the number and they set up a time for me to call back with the number. I called the big time accounting firm and was told that they hadn't gotten a State ID Number for me because I hadn't asked them to do it. I told them that the reason I had hired them was for their expertise and how was I to know what I needed, that was supposed to be their responsibility!

I fired them and called The Texas Employment Commission and told them that I didn't have a Texas Tax ID Number. The bureaucrat at the Employment Commission told me to send him copies of my employment records starting from the first employee I had hired. I sent in the records and about a week later, I

TEXAS OASIS, This title is the result of my annual contest to name one of my prints, Parts of Texas would never have been settled if it hadn't been for the windmill providing a man made oasis.

received a statement, which was for the unemployment tax that I owed plus interest and penalties for not filing, penalties for filing late and interest on all of that prorated from the day I hired my first employee!

Although the original tax owed was less than a thousand dollars, the penalties and interest came to around thirty thousand dollars! I was in shock and called the bureaucrat and asked for mercy, since I had been unaware of the State Tax and that I didn't have the money. The bureaucrat had no sympathy and hinted that they could seize my property and assets.

I told him that I couldn't work with him and demanded that I speak to his supervisor (I had read somewhere that I had the right to appeal to a higher authority) The bureaucrat told me that his supervisor was lots tougher than he was and that I would be better off not to deal with his supervisor.

I insisted on talking to his supervisor anyway and set up an appointment. I got no where with the supervisor who indeed, was tougher than the first bureaucrat and he accused me of stalling, at which point, I insisted on talking to the supervisor's, supervisor.

I went through the supervisor's, supervisor's, supervisor and was finally told that I would have talk to the "Chief of Tax". I called the Chief of Tax and his secretary asked me for my name. The Chief of Tax picked up the phone and said " Hey man, how's the Art Business?" He told me he was one of my customers and asked me what he could do for me!

I poured out my story and he said "If you were trying to get out of paying taxes you wouldn't have a Federal Tax ID. You just hired a sloppy accounting firm. Those big

HEALTH CAMP has been on the Waco traffic circle since 1949 and the name seems to be coming back around to popularity again, what with the Atkins diet and all! Waco has one of the few if not the only active traffic circles left in Texas that still looks like stepping back in time!

shot firms do lousy work and you should sue them for malpractice! By the way the State Tax is deductible from the Federal Tax so you paid the right amount of money but it went to the wrong place" He said that I would have to pay the original tax since the State didn't have a process for getting their share from the Feds, but that he would eliminate all of the penalties and interest and that I could pay the original tax in installments and that I would be sent a statement that I could use to deduct the State Tax I had paid from my Federal Taxes and that it would be a "wash".

I shudder to think of what would have been the case if I hadn't fought my way up the bureaucratic ladder to finally talk to someone who actually had the authority to say something other than no.

Just one more case of my having good luck with my bad luck!

COWBOY CORSAGE, In 1997, while preparing for our annual open house, we picked some wildflowers from the field behind the house and made some centerpieces. After looking at this centerpiece for a couple of days, I decided it would make a nice painting.

BRUCE THE COWGOOSE

Not long after Martha and I moved to the Ranch a friend named Rod Spivey gave me two Geese and a week or so after bringing the two Geese home, I began to doubt his motives. It became apparent that instead of a gift it was more of a joke! These two creatures were the most hostile things that I had ever encountered. They attacked and terrorized our dogs. A bird has knuckles on its wings right where the primary flight feathers are based and the Geese would punch our dogs unmercifully.

These two marauders would run up under our horses bellies, when they were eating the feed we had put out for them and pinch the horses until the Horses abandoned their food, leaving the Geese to eat the Horse feed.

When I was feeding our Cattle, the demonic pair would come and pinch the Cattle on their noses until the Cattle moved on. Anyone visiting us would have to deal with these two feathered fiends, pinching with their beaks and beating with their wings.

All of our animals put up with this harassment for a good while but our ten Longhorns finally had enough and decided to end their reign of terror. The ten Longhorns surrounded the two Geese and lowered their horns and took turns charging at the Geese. The Geese escaped by flying straight up in the air, which was the first time I had seen them use their wings for something other than battering rams and I decided to teach them how to fly better.

Fortunately for Martha and I, the Geese seemed to like us and didn't try to abuse us, but followed us everywhere we walked. The Geese were much better watch dogs than the dogs and no one got close without a chorus of squawking to announce their arrival.

We named the Geese "Goosie Lucy" and "Brucie Goosie"! When Martha and I went walking in the morning, the Geese would follow us, so I would run towards one of our stock tanks flapping my arms and the Geese would run after me flapping their wings until they started flying at which time they would fly over my head and land in the stock tank.

My plan was to get them flying well enough that, hopefully, they would fly off and migrate with one of the wild flocks that occasionally passed over the ranch.

A couple of years passed and one night, Goosie Lucy got caught by Coyotes and Brucie was left as the lone Goose. Apparently the Coyotes, being wild and hungry, were willing to take a beating to get a meal and Goosie Lucy's terror tactics hadn't worked so well on them.

Well, after a period of mourning, Brucie Goose took up with one of our dogs named Bear and went everywhere Bear went. Brucie Goose became submissive to Bear and didn't try to terrorize him like he had done when Goosie Lucy was alive. Bear would crawl up under my pickup truck to get out of the hot sun and Brucie Goose would crawl

G Boutwell

under the truck and try to cuddle up with Bear. Bear would grab Brucie Goose's head in her mouth, without hurting him and would drag Brucie Goose out from under the truck, drag him about 50 feet away from the truck, let go of Brucie Goose's head and run at top speed for the truck.

Brucie Goose would fly back to the truck and arrive there at the same time as Bear and the two would repeat the process over and over.

When I went to feed my cattle in the morning, my two dogs, Bear and Lucky would run after our Longhorn cattle, to drive them up to the truck, where I was waiting to feed them. Brucie Goose couldn't resist trying to help the dogs and he would fly along side of my Longhorn cattle, squawking. I wish I had taken a movie of this crazy bird herding cattle because it was a totally hilarious sight.

About a year later, stray dogs caught Brucie Goose and killed him (We knew that Dogs had done the deed because we found his mutilated body and Coyotes would have never left a kill, they totally consume what they kill) and surprisingly we mourned for him because we had unintentionally become attached to him. ◆

COWDOG CABANA, Although this isn't the truck in the above story, I thought it would be appropriate! This old Chevrolet Pickup is one that I've used in several paintings over the past several years. I always go to the Stamford Cowboy Reunion and I don't remember a year when this truck wasn't parked beside the entrance to the Rodeo Arena. I think most of the Artists who participate in the Western Art Show have done a painting that included this truck, or they have at least photographed it, with that idea in mind. Although I don't remember if I've ever met the owner, I've been told that he works at the reunion each year. Each year this truck gets a fresh paint job, right over any dirt that might be on it, with a big paint brush! This truck has got to be one of the most aesthetically interesting I've seen and restoring it to like new condition would be the equivalent of destroying a great work of Art! The dogs weren't really under this truck but that's where any ranch dog in Texas wants to be. Certainly it's where you will find our dogs on most hot summer days!

TRIP TO THE CLOUDS

Martha and I decided to get out of the Texas summer heat and I booked the Western Heritage Art Show in Littleton Colorado. My Uncle Frank had retired and was living in nearby Aurora, so we combined the show with a visit to my Aunt Alpa and Uncle Frank (I had stayed a Summer with Frank and Alpa in Vermont when I was 12, a story about that, later in the book)

On Monday, after the show closed, we decided to drive to the top of Mt. Evans which boasted to have the highest road in the United States (14,256 feet) . The view going up the mountain was fabulous and we stopped frequently to take pictures.

We ate a picnic lunch at a roadside park, by crystal clear Mirror Lake and were pestered by Chipmunks and Gray Jays wanting a handout.

As we climbed farther up the mountain, we reached the tree line and the view improved but the barren landscape wasn't as pretty. The road suddenly narrowed and there was no guard rail and although we were on the mountain side of the road, it was still scary to realize that it was at least 1000 feet down from the edge of the road. Mirror Lake looked like a little blue dot below.

To make matters worse, we then drove into a cloud and could barely see the road, which by now was partially covered with ice and snow was falling to boot!. Martha was openly panic stricken and I wasn't doing much better. Martha said "turn around, we've gone far enough, let's get out of here", I said, "I would love to turn around but this motor home is longer than the width of the road so we have no choice but to go to the top". (there is a visitor center and parking lot at the top of Mt. Evans.)

Meanwhile, we inched along at

BACK PORCH ANNIE Martha and her Mother, spent untold hours making Raggedy Anne and Andy dolls as Christmas Presents for Valerie and Kimberlee. I found Raggedy Anne sitting on the back porch sunning herself and couldn't resist painting this!

about three miles per hour while cars with Colorado plates came flying by us, probably uttering disparaging remarks about Texans. Finally, we hit a break in the clouds and the snow stopped falling and we breathed a little sigh of relief. We were almost to the top, when like a miracle, a parking area appeared and I pulled the motor home off the road and focused my thoughts on the harrowing trip we might face going back down on the "drop off" side of the road.

I got out and took a few steps and could hardly breathe because of the thin freezing air at that altitude. I struggled my way back to the motor home and we sat there for a while gathering our thoughts. We decided not to go on to the visitor center, which was about a half mile farther up the mountain. We didn't care that we didn't reach the top of the mountain at that point, so we inched our way back down.

I was terrified about driving the motor home just inches from a sheer drop off on the right side of the road (what if the pavement broke away when we were so close to the edge?) I decided, safety was more important than courtesy, so, I drove in the middle of the road, forcing the oncoming vehicles to almost scrape the side of the mountain as they passed. I was afraid to apply my brakes very firmly on the icy road so I drove in low gear and rode the brakes gently to keep my speed at about 5 miles per hour, until we got down out of the clouds and back to the tree line where the road was wider.

I pulled over to let the brakes cool and the long line of cars that were behind us passed by and several of the folks in the cars flashed obscene gestures at us. We eased down in low gear, stopping frequently, to let the brakes cool and finally made it to level ground where I was tempted to get out and kiss the ground! ⬩

SHADE TREE MARKET, This could be anyplace in Texas in the summer. These two entrepreneurs were beside the railroad track in Luling, Texas and twenty five years after I photographed them, an elderly lady from Luling told me their names!

HILL COUNTY, Named for its location, "Hill County", Texas. I've always loved old barns, probably because my Grandmother used to tell me, I acted like I was raised in one!. Ray & Betty Sawyer, let me park my motor home in their driveway when I showed at the Bond's Alley Art Show and gave me a tour of the area and I found lots of Painting subjects like this one above.

BUCKAROOS

This Painting was done from a trip to a ranch at Pawhuska Oklahoma that was owned by Steve Adams. I did several Paintings from this trip which were all purchased by Steve.

I was looking thru my photographs from the ranch and seeing these two young boys on horseback triggered a memory of the summer when I was 12. My Uncle Frank (my Fathers oldest Brother) had bought a farm in Vermont and I was sent up there to spend the Summer. There were two boys, Kerry and Kevin Keenan, that were about my age that lived up the road from my Uncle's farm, so my Uncle took me to their Dairy Farm and I became friends with both boys.

Every afternoon the cows would automatically come in from the pasture to the milk barn for milking. The Keenans had several horses and we boys decided that we would pretend that the cows had to be rounded up and driven to the barn. We would run up to the back of a horse, place both hands on the horses rump and "leapfrog" up onto the horse, "Indian style" and ride them bareback down to the pasture and round up the cattle, "just like in the movies!" Since the cattle came into the barn each day by habit we were very successful in our round ups and cattle drives.

Later in life the first time I rode horseback with a saddle and reins, I found it incredibly easy compared to riding bareback! ⬥

BUCKAROOS, These two young cowboys were the sons of "Skeet Rasberry", one of the cowboys on Steve Adam's ranch, at Pawhuska, Oklahoma and were tending to the herd

143

COWBOY FOR A DAY

Gardner and Mary Ann Parker invited me to come to their Anchor X Ranch in the hill country near Lampassas, Texas and I ended up doing several Paintings from the trips I made there to take photographs.

On one of the trips, I was introduced to Morris Van who managed the ranch and I assumed from his humble demeanor that he was a hired hand (boy was I wrong). Morris offered to give me a tour of the operation and we got into his rather beat up pickup truck and drove around.

We would cross a cattle guard and Morris would tell me that either he owned this ranch or who did and that he was in partnership with them. After crossing several more cattle guards, I began to realize that Morris was the owner of a considerable amount of land and managed much, much more and was an extremely successful rancher.

I made the comment that I had assumed from his beat up truck, that he was just one of the cowboys and Morris laughed and said he preferred that folks saw him that way. He told me that he was born on the ranch and hoped to die there and being a cowboy was all he ever wanted to be. Morris told me that he could afford a better truck but that would be wasteful, because the truck we were in was not worn out yet.

If anyone sees the trucks we use on our ranch, it will be obvious that I took Morris's advice to heart. Morris told me that he would call me when they were going to round up and be working cattle, so I could come and ride with them.

It was a hot July day (100 plus degrees) when we saddled up and rode out, to round up several hundred head of cattle from one of the more remote pastures, at a ranch

DRINKIN WIT DA BOYS These Hereford Calves and the water tank were at the Anchor X Ranch near Lampassas, Texas (the Ranch in the story above.) . For a closer look at the water tank, look at the following page!

144

COUNTRY CANTINA Stock tanks like this one at the Anchor X Ranch are quite common in Texas. During a heat wave, a stock tank often becomes a lifesaver for many wild creatures such as these Bobwhite Quail.

Morris called Indian Bluffs. Morris put me on a mare that he said was his best cutting horse and told me "if you want to take pictures, just pull the reins over the saddle horn and she will stand perfectly still like a statue and you can shoot all the pictures you want. If you want to be a cowboy and herd cattle, she loves to work cattle and knows just what to do, just let go of the reins and hang on to the saddle horn and enjoy the ride!" Morris told me that he had no doubt in his mind that this mare could out perform any of those "Fancy Rodeo Cutting Horses".

Morris told me that his cow dogs would do most of the real work and that our job was mostly to guide the dogs. Morris, his two sons, two other cowboys and I rode up to the

COWBOY COMMUNION This is one of those horse before the cart Paintings where I wanted to use the sunburst in a Painting so I came up with an idea to justify it. The Cowboy is Morris Vann of Lampassas who gave me the privilege of riding in a round up!

remote pasture and the dogs started rousting the cattle out of the brush. Soon, there were several hundred cattle bunched up and we started moving them toward the working pens that were a few miles away. I shot lots of pictures and a couple of times when some of the cattle started straying out to the side, I could feel the mare's anxiousness, so I would let go of the reins and hang on and she would dash back and forth and run the straying cattle back into the herd. I was glad to have the saddle horn to hang onto, as I could have never hung on if I had been riding bareback like I did when I was twelve!

One incredible moment in the cattle drive was when a large bull broke out of the herd and headed for the brush. Two of the cow dogs came out of nowhere at lightning speed and caught up with the bull in a matter of seconds. One of the dogs leaped into the air and grabbed one of the bull's ears and hung on while the bull flopped his head back and forth with the incredibly tough dog flopping around, still hanging on to the ear. Finally, the pain was getting to the bull and he lowered his head, at which time the second dog jumped up and grabbed the bull by the nose, latched on and went "dead weight." The most sensitive part of a bull is his nose and it didn't take long for the bull to drop to the ground to relieve the weight of the

LUNCH LINE AT THE ANCHOR X Morris Vann, the manager of the Anchor X Ranch loaned me a jeep to explore the ranch. As I drove up to one of the more remote pastures, these cattle heard the familiar sound of the engine and lined up in hopes of being fed!

dog on his nose. Morris rode up to the dogs and bull and told the dogs to "let go". The dogs obeyed and backed up a little and barked at the bull, who, now with no fight left in him, got up and headed back to the herd. I'm still amazed at how, two fifty pound dogs so quickly subdued a two thousand pound bull.

I shot more pictures, let go of the reins a couple more times and went on a couple more wild rides. When we came over the top of the hill overlooking the working pens I got the bright idea to ride ahead and climb up on the entrance gate to get some shots of the herd coming into the pens.

Although I did shoot some really good pictures, I was in a state of panic when the mass of cattle began bumping up against the fence and the gate post I was clinging to, was waving back and forth. If that gate had went down I would have been ground to a pulp! Fortunately, the post held and I'm here to tell the story!

After the herd was in the pens, we took a break, ate some lunch and the dogs laid down under one of the trucks. Morris told me, "man, you are a natural in the saddle, most people have to ride a long time before they ride as well as you do!, I really didn't expect you to ever let go of the reins" I told him about my bareback riding as a kid and how having a saddle sure made it easier! The only two cowboy hats in the group were worn by Morris and myself, the other cowboys all wore baseball caps. I commented to one of the cowboys that his dress (tee shirt, ball cap, sneakers and mirror sunglasses) didn't quite fit my impression of a cowboy, to which

SPARE WHEELS I found these wagon wheels leaning on a Fence near the old Rock House at the Anchor X Ranch west of Lampassas, Texas and wondered about the stories they could tell if they were able!

DUB BROWN "Probably the best cowboy I know" according to Rancher Morris Vann of Lampasas, Texas. This scene was at the Indian Bluffs Ranch in the separating pens on the day I got to sit in the saddle and be one of the cowboys!

he replied "western clothes cost too much and we ain't makin a movie"
    All but two of the horses were

unsaddled and turned loose and the remaining two were ridden by Morris and one of his sons, to move

the cattle into the various pens. Some cattle needed to be vaccinated, some needed to be branded, large

DUST BANDITS This Painting is the result of my getting up on the corral gate and taking pictures as the cattle were being driven in to the separating pens and I ate a lot of dust in the process!

THE BIG SQUEEZE That's Rancher Morris Van of Lampassas on the right, his two sons, center and the late "Dub" Brown, a lifelong cowboy, on the left and the White Faced Hereford coming into the chute was about to receive a vaccination and an ear tag to keep the flies away.

LAZY AFTERNOON In my observations, I've found that wild animals can sense danger or know if a stranger means them no harm. Many times, I've been able to photograph and observe wild animals at extremely close range while they were fully aware of my presence. This painting is from the Anchor X Ranch between Burnet and Lampasas, and thanks to Gardner and Mary Ann Parker I have had the privilege of roaming around and finding a wealth of things to paint!

calves needed to be separated from their Mothers to stop them from nursing so that the Mother cow could recover from the physical stress of nursing, young bulls would be neutered and others would be taken to market.

The cowboy that told me that they weren't making a movie was on foot in one of the pens, when one of the cows charged him, he quickly vaulted over the fence, out of harms way, turned to me, pointing to his sneakers, said "no way I could'da done that in cowboy boots"

I spent most of the remaining time taking pictures and at about four in the afternoon, when all the work was done, one of the cowboys said, "I'm glad we didn't bet real money on you, none of us thought a city boy like you could handle the heat, we figured you would call it quits before lunch!" I invited him to come help me set up and stand for two days in August, at the Salado Art Fair (usually over 100 degrees) and I said "cowboys aren't the only Texans that are tough!

As I was getting ready to leave I told them that I had really enjoyed the day and that it was probably just another hard days work for them, to which, one of the cowboys replied, "there's nothing on earth I would rather be doing!" I now understood why I enjoyed their company so much, we all had something in common, we loved our work!

Morris paid me a genuine compliment as I was leaving, he said, "you are about as good a hand as I've seen and you are welcome to come help out any time"!

A HERO THAT WOULDN'T DIE

Windmills have always been a favorite subject for me. They were a lifeline for the early settlers and with the invention of the electric pump, seemed destined to becoming an obsolete part of our vanishing rural scene. Now, due to our energy problems, many of the old Windmill companies have resumed production and we will have these graceful machines to enjoy for many more years. This fine Windmill is on the Anchor X Ranch, the scene of the story above!

EXPLORING A DIFFERENT WORLD

I met Chuck Naiser somewhere around 1975, (I really can't remember exactly when, but since he bought my first color prints in 1975, I assume it's been at least that long)

If there is a more avid fisherman than Chuck, I would be surprised! Chuck invited me to come down to Rockport and go fishing with him and since I had always wanted to see the back bays and other places on the coast that can't be seen from any road, I jumped all over his offer.

Frankly fishing was secondary to the opportunity to look for new things to paint. The coastal marsh is an incredibly beautiful area and when you get away from the signs of civilization it becomes timeless.

Chuck lived in West Columbia where he was in the insurance business to make enough money to pay for his fishing habit. Chuck has a house on a canal that empties into Copano Bay near Rockport on the Texas coast.

We got in Chuck's "Boston Whaler" boat and headed out before dawn. We headed straight into the sunrise which was really a great one and when we got out to the inter-coastal waterway we turned left up the channel for several miles.

We stopped and fished (I did more photographing than fishing) at different locations several times and I was amazed at how clear the water was in comparison to what you see near the roads close to the shore. We stopped for lunch and sat on a big driftwood log and ate sandwiches. As we were getting ready to fish some more, Chuck looked out into the gulf and saw a storm building, so he turned on the weather radio in his boat and the forecast was not in our favor. The weather service was issuing a "Small Craft Warning". Chuck said that we had better get moving if we were going to outrun the storm, so we got in the boat and

SMALL CRAFT WARNING This was inspired on a fishing trip near Rockport, Texas, where a squall can come up with almost no warning and it's best to head for land. We couldn't outrun this storm and got totally soaked before we got into port.

hightailed it up the channel. We were putting some distance between us and the storm, but the problem was, that we were going to have to make a sharp right turn to get back into Copano Bay and several miles of our route after the right turn would be in deep water. We no sooner made the turn, when the storm hit us with driving rain and high winds and we were running in six foot swells. At this point Chuck told me that in order to get out of our predicament we would have to get the boat on top of the swells. Chuck said "this isn't going to be fun, but I know what I'm doing, so stand up and hang on real tight" Chuck opened the throttle, wide open and we went over the top of one of the six foot swells and dove right into the next swell and got really wet. Chuck repeated the process from a little different angle and we dove into another swell.

After a couple more attempts, the boat went over the top of a swell and landed squarely on top of the next swell and Chuck held the throttle

WINNER LOSES This is from a fishing trip that I took with Chuck Naiser. We left Rockport and went along the bay side of Matagorda Island where the water is crystal clear. There are three Speckled Trout in the foreground, eyeing the lure that is moving thru the water and the fish that grabs this prize is the loser!

CHASING THE GLOW I went fishing with Mike Lairsen in the Laguna Madre near Rio Hondo, Texas and as we were heading for the open water following a couple of other boats, he asked me what my next fishing Painting would be and I replied "you're looking at it". The boat we were following didn't appeal to me so I substituted a boat from another fishing trip near Rockport with Chuck Naiser. I had done a similar, much smaller Painting earlier that I hadn't published and had donated it to the Gulf Coast Conservation Association for a fundraising auction. and I was reminded of it as I watched from Mike's boat.

156

wide open and the we skipped like a flat rock, from the top of one swell to the tops of the others. We were moving really fast and the boat was literally airborne between the tops of the swells and although it was an incredibly rough, bouncing ride, we quickly got out of the deep water and the ride got smoother as we got into more shallow water and the driving wind and rain seemed almost insignificant. After this experience, most folks would have never left shore again but I went fishing several more times with Chuck and several of his friends and shot tons of photographs and even caught a fish or two.

One memorable trip with Chuck happened without any problems, the weather was perfect, I got lots of good photographs, the fish were biting and we had material for one of those "Fish Stories" that fishermen brag about.

We had a whole mess of Speckled Trout in the live tank of Chuck's boat

STARTING OUT RIGHT I've gone fishing at Rockport several times with Chuck Naiser and he always tells me how good the fishing has been, but it never seems to be that way when I go with him. On this trip, things were different, Chuck stepped out of the boat and caught a nice Redfish on the first cast; this set the pace for the rest of the morning and gave Chuck's previous fish stories credibility!

and, as we started heading back Chuck got on the radio and called his wife Margueritte and told her to light the burner under the deep fryer. When we pulled up to the dock, Marguerite had Chuck's "Secret Batter Ingredients" laid out on a table on the dock. We pulled up to the dock and immediately Chuck pulled each live fish from the tank, cut their heads off, trimmed them, rolled them in the flour and "Secret Spices" and dropped them into the deep fryer. (For those of you who worry about the pain inflicted on the fish, fish have no "Pain Nerves" so there is no suffering.) Chuck turned to me and said, "look around, do you see any Sea Gulls?" I looked around and not a gull was to be seen. Chuck said "watch this" as he picked up all of

MUD ISLAND In March I went fishing with my friend Chuck Naiser in Rockport. We met artist Herb Booth and his son Jimmy, and all went searching for fish in Chuck's boat. We tried hard but the fish just weren't biting and soon my attention wandered to the patterns of the mud flats and water!

HIGH HOPES This fellow is Chuck Naiser who introduced me to bay fishing at Rockport, Texas. I don't believe there is anyone who likes fishing more. Chuck has shown me every bay in Aransas County and sometimes we have even caught fish.

the fish scraps and tossed them up into the air over the water. Out of nowhere, sea gulls appeared and not one fish scrap hit the water! The fish were ready to eat and we sat there on the dock and ate our fill. I had never had better tasting fish in my whole life! It is amazing how much better fish tastes, when it's only been dead seconds before being cooked!

Years later in 2001 I decided to produce a Texas Coastal Calendar and wanted to photograph the endangered Whooping Cranes that winter near Rockport, so I called the Rockport Chamber of Commerce and obtained a list of Whooping Crane Guides.

I didn't know anything about any of the guides listed, so I called Chuck to see if he would recommend one of them. By this time Chuck had gotten out of the insurance business and had become a full time "Fishing Guide". Chuck asked me when I wanted to photograph the Whooping Cranes and when I told him the date, he said, "I'm not booked that day and I'll be glad to take you out, I know where I can get you close to some birds"

I was to meet Chuck at the boat ramp at Goose Island State Park at about 7:00 am and I got there a little early and as I was standing by the water I saw a flock of White Pelicans circling the bay and they swooped in and landed in the water not twenty feet from where I stood and I shot a bunch of photographs. Chuck arrived at 7:00 sharp and we piled into his boat and headed down the channel.

After we had gone about ten miles we pulled up beside several large boats that had lots of people on board, armed with binoculars and telephoto lenses. The Whooping Cranes were about a quarter of a mile away in the marsh and were barely visible. I liked the terrain and

DIE HARD I was supposed to go fishing with Chuck Naiser at Rockport but a storm was brewing and the water was too rough to fish so we decided to cancel. Later I was driving along Fulton Beach and was amazed by this fellow out on a pier, seemingly oblivious to the waves that were crashing across the pier. He must have wanted to fish more than we did.

MURPHY'S LAW That's Cecil Duncan on the left and Chuck Naiser on the right and we were fishing out of Rockport, Texas and frankly no records were broken that day! This has got to be the most honest fishing painting that's ever been done and if you can't relate to this, then all I can say is "you just ain't never been fishing"!

WORKING ON A FULL HOUSE This Painting is a composition from several fishing trips to the backwater bays of the Texas coast. Chuck Naiser is the fisherman and was the first to introduce me to bay fishing and later the first to introduce me to saltwater fly fishing. Later, I was given a refresher course by Bud Rowland and Del Fankhauser which got me in the mood to paint another fishing scene. There are two Redfish and two Speckled Trout on the stringer, the light is fading fast but maybe there is time catch one more and a Full House will beat Two Pair!

took some photos but got no worthwhile shots of the Whooping Cranes.

I was feeling pretty disapointed and thought I had wasted a day, when Chuck grinned and asked me, "getting any good pictures?" I said "not really" Chuck pointed to the big boats beside us and said "those are all of the Whooping Crane Guides, they will sit there for a while, then take all those folks back to the dock, that's what you would have gotten for your money, now lets go get close to some birds!"

We ran down the channel a few miles and Chuck turned the boat into one of the shallow bays and turned off the motor. I could see about ten Whooping Cranes that were about a half of a mile away and Chuck said " we have the wind to our back and it will push us toward the Whooping Cranes".

Chuck told me to lay down on the front of the boat with my camera ready to shoot pictures and said "this may take half an hour but we are going to drift right up to the Cranes. If we are real still they will let us get within twenty feet of them and then they will start walking to keep that distance between us."

Sure enough, in about half an hour, we were close enough to see their eyelashes! I shot pictures taking care to not move a muscle except for the finger that was on the shutter of the camera!

The Cranes started walking down the edge of the marsh and we drifted along behind them taking more pictures until the Cranes turned into a narrow inlet that was too narrow for the boat. Chuck fired up the motor and we headed for two more bays and repeated the drifting process, each time and I shot photos until I ran out of film! 🖤

ADDRESSING THE FLOCK I was waiting at the Goose Island State Park boat landing for Chuck Naiser to arrive with his boat to go looking for Whooping Cranes. At first light, I watched these White Pelicans fly closer and closer until they landed in the water right in front of me. I wondered if the one going in a different direction from the others was the leader or just a non conformist!

MAJESTY IN THE MARSH Whooping Cranes were close to extinction but thanks to conservation efforts, they are on the rebound. Most of the Whooping Crane population winters in the coastal marshes of Texas near Rockport at the Aransas Wildlife Refuge. Thanks to Chuck Naiser "one of the best guides on the Texas coast", I had the priveledge of getting so close to the Whooping Cranes that I could see their eyelashes!

These two Paintings are previously unpublished:

Left: Small islands made of Oyster Shell are covered with yucca and cactus which seems out of place out in the bay.

Right: This scene is in early morning near the road to Port Aransas where the offshore Oil Rigs are assembled.

TAILS AND SAILS

I was walking along the shore of the bay after the Rockport Art Festival and noticed some Redfish feeding in the shallow water with their tails out of the water at about the same time that I noticed a small sailboat farther out in the bay and this Painting and it's title immediately came to mind!

165

A LASTING TRADITION

In 1981, I was accepted to show my work at the Cowboy Reunion, Western Art Show at Stamford, Texas. The Cowboy Reunion started in 1930 and is a legendary amatuer Rodeo that pioneered many of the Rodeo events that are famous today.

At the time, the focus of my work was Western Art and I was honored to be accepted in this show which featured many prominent Western Artists. I was showing my work in Billings, Montana at the American, Canadian Art Classic and I had packed up my work on Sunday evening and driven strait thru to Stamford without sleeping!

I have shown my work at the Stamford Cowboy Reunion each year since (30 years at this writing) and have done many Paintings, based on my experiences from the Reunion. The following Paintings are just a few of the works I've done that were inspired at the Reunion! ⚜

FLYING COLORS

When I was asked to produce a Painting to be featured on the cover of the official program for the Stamford Cowboy Reunion, I thought this was appropriate since it was inspired at the Reunion. The owner of this Original later donated it to the Reunion and it was auctioned as a fund raiser for the Reunion and brought a record price.

DAYDREAMING

As I watched this little fellow on his father's horse at the Stamford Cowboy Reunion, I tried to imagine the things he was thinking; was he chasing bandits; winning a championship rodeo; riding the pony express? I remembered some of the daydreams I'd had as a child and wondered, why we seem to fantasize less as we grow up. It occurred to me that, at a time such as childhood, when we have the least amount of control over our lives, we use our imagination much more. Because I make my living using my imagination, I sometimes take for granted, the great release this state of mind can provide and I wonder how much better life could be for everyone if simple daydreaming were encouraged more.

COLOR GUARD This is from the parade at the Stamford Cowboy Reunion, although I moved the gas station a little closer than it exists in reality. This parade is an annual event that includes practically everyone in the area that has a horse! I have enjoyed this parade for many years and many of the characters that I have included in so many of my paintings were photographed at this parade!

FRONT ROW SEATS   This is another Painting inspired at the Stamford Cowboy Reunion. I was wandering around the grounds, taking pictures and found this practice arena where the Cowboys were practicing under the scrutiny of their peers. Although I shot my reference photographs at least ten years earlier, I waited to do the Painting until 1997 and published it in late 1997 as one of the pages on my 1998 Texas Cowboy Calendar!

RODEO STARS   I was in the staging area for the Fourth of July parade at the Stamford Cowboy Reunion, when I happened on this cowboy sitting on his trailer in a locked stare with his horse. He was decked out in Texas Flag attire and his horse was also dressed for the occasion but something was missing. His trailer was light blue and his truck was gray and I put off the Painting until I saw a truck and trailer painted up like the Texas Flag pass me on the highway and I knew instantly what the Painting needed!

IN TOWN FOR THE REUNION   The Grand Theater, built in 1936, is on the courthouse square in Stamford, Texas, home of the famous Texas Cowboy Reunion. The western movie Bandolero was filmed in 1968 near Brackettville, Texas. Recognize anyone in the cars? This theater is on the Fourth of July parade route on the downtown Stamford square and I sat on the square in my motor home and painted all but the cars on my kitchen table in the motor home.

LENDING A HAND This was at the Stamford Cowboy Reunion, as I was watching the activities behind the arena in preparation for the Rodeo. This little boy and his Father are the same ones shown in my Painting "Daydreaming" which is shown five pages back in this book! I have found more inspiring subjects observing the preparation for the Rodeo than I have found in the actual Rodeo!

LUEDERS FALLS   This 20 foot high waterfall is on the Clear Fork of the Brazos River at Lueders, Texas which is north east of Abilene, close to Stamford. There are two sets of falls about 30 feet apart and the upper falls are barely visible from below the lower falls so I moved them up a bit to show better in the Painting. These waterfalls are on private property and very few of the locals even know about them. I found these falls in the "Texas Whitewater" kayaking book and since I didnt want to take a 17 mile kayak trip, I tried to get directions in Lueders, but no one knew where the falls were. I went to the Art Show at the Stamford Cowboy Reunion and asked several people who had no idea that the falls even existed. Finally, I asked the security guard at the Reunion and he told me that he had fished there most of his life and gave me detailed directions, so I included a fisherman in the Painting!

A QUICK TOUR OF TEXAS

These final pages show some of my favorite paintings and start at the Texas Panhandle and run clockwise around the state of Texas!

TEXAS PANHANDLE

PASSING MAJESTY
Palo Duro Canyon in the Texas Panhandle is the nations second largest canyon! This view is from one of the many hiking trails in Palo Duro Canyon State Park!

PALO DURO PANORAMA
Palo Duro Canyon cuts an enormous gash across the otherwise flat Texas Panhandle. The colors and forms revealed by millions of years of wind and water erosion are quite spectacular. I put the horse and rider on the ridge just to show the scale of this wonder of nature.

THE CONOCO TOWER STATION and U Drop Inn Cafe were built in 1936 in Shamrock, Texas on historic Route 66. It was considered to be the finest building between Oklahoma City and Amarillo! It is now a museum and Shamrock's Chamber of Commerce

TEXAS' FIRST PHILLIPS 66 This Station is in McLean, Texas on historic Route 66, and was built in 1929 and operated for over 50 years. This was the First Phillips 66 station ever built in Texas and the first service station on historic Route 66 to be restored.

CACTUS INN is on historic Route 66 in the Texas Panhandle town of McLean. The big tall cactus is a real eye catcher!

COWBOY MOTEL is located in Amarillo, Texas at 3619 East Amarillo Boulevard (old Route 66!) I couldn't resist putting real cowboys hanging out beneath the sign!

NORTH TEXAS

This is my idea of how a day should begin! "Up early with a nice hot cup of coffee and some good company to watch the sunrise while contemplating all of our blessings! After such a great start, it's hard for the day to go any other way!" The porch is near Red Oak, Texas the barn is at Fairy, Texas and the cowboy and dog were at the Stamford Cowboy Reunion!

BAR-L is located at 308 13th Street in Wichita Falls, Texas and is famous for their ribs and a drink called the "Red Draft", a mixture of tomato juice and beer. The Bar-L is one of only 2 places in Texas that will bring a beer to your car due to being grandfathered when the law changed.

WINDTHORST, TEXAS is on U.S. 281 about 25 miles south of Wichita Falls and this store stopped me in my tracks as I was heading for Amarillo. I replaced some newer vehicles with more appropriate ones, including the 1957 Pontiac we used to own!

THE LAST PICTURE SHOW The National Theater, in downtown Graham, Texas, was built in 1919 and remodeled in 1939. "The Last Picture Show" was filmed at Archer City, Texas, just north of Graham, in 1971. That's the cast out front in the cars they drove in the movie.

ROSSTON, TEXAS is on Farm Road 922, west of Valley View and northwest of Denton. I was told about Rosston and decided to go and see for myself. That's owner Nick Muller and his mother sitting on the porch. Y'all stop by, these are right friendly folks!

WISE COUNTY COURTHOUSE This Romanesque Revival style Courthouse is on the Decatur square and was designed by J. Riely Gordon and built in 1896. This Courthouse is very similar to those in Waxahachie, Sulphur Springs, Gonzales and Giddings.

CRUISIN' GREENVILLE AVENUE The Granada Theater is on lower Greenville Avenue in Dallas and was built in 1948. The movie "JFK" was filmed in Dallas in 1991 but those are not the actors in the Lincoln. You never know who will be cruisin' Greenville Avenue!

DOWNTOWN CLARKSVILLE, TEXAS This is the northwest corner of the square as it may have looked in the 1950's. Jack Holt of the Chamber of Commerce gave me the names of the businesses. The Blackmon's Pharmacy sign is still there and I guessed on the others.

EAST TEXAS

DEEP IN THE WOODS OF TEXAS
This is Dogwood time in the Big Thicket of East Texas, a pine forest as large as New England and always overlooked by those unenlightened clods who describe Texas as a desert wasteland.

EARLY BIRD BREAKFAST
I found this row of old buildings on the outskirts of Pineland, Texas and my imagination went into high gear. The Sunglo Feed sign suggested early morning and I created the rest, added the cars, trucks and people and breakfast is served!

LINDSEY STORE is at Jonesville, Texas on Farm Road 134, just west of Waskom near the Louisiana border. The inside of this store is probably one of the most interesting you will find and was used as a setting in a Walt Disney movie.

DOGWOOD TRAILS Dogwood trees explode into bloom all over East Texas each spring and tourists come from all over to marvel at their beauty. Martha and I took a week in the spring to tour East Texas and see some of Texas that we hadn't seen before.

C. E. ROGERS & SON Store opened in 1889 and it's appearance has changed very little. It was the oldest business in Rusk County when it closed recently. It is located in the Stewart Community on Fm 782 between Longview and Kilgore, Texas.

SABINE PASS The Texas, Louisiana State Line is in the middle of the water in this picture and although the Lighthouse is actually located in Louisiana, it was built in 1906 to serve only Texas ports and efforts are underway to restore and preserve it.

179

PELICANS AND PATTERNS I was driving on the causeway that connects Port Isabel to South Padre Island when I spotted these Brown Pelicans near the base of the causeway at Port Isabel. I pulled up and parked and walked down to where they were and took several photographs, which I used for reference for this painting.

FIXER UPPER I found this old Shrimp Boat in Rockport, waiting for repairs and was spellbound by the flaking red paint. I removed the building that was behind it and replaced it with the bay as a background.

SURF SKIMMING I have always been fascinated by Skimmers, at first glance these birds seem to have no eyes or feet. This is because their eyes are the same color as their black caps and their feet tuck up under their feathers like the landing gear on a Jet Liner.

PORT ARANSAS LIGHTHOUSE I was in a duck blind in the mangrove swamp behind the 1857 Aransas Pass Lighthouse and watched the sunrise and took several pictures as the light changed. Winter colors here are only brown if there has been a hard freeze.

WIND RIPPLES The sand dunes at Padre Island are possibly the best on the Texas coast and I've spent hours exploring the constantly changing patterns, sculpted by the ever present sea breeze!

181

OCTILLO TWILIGHT I have always wanted to drive the river road along the Rio Grande, up river from Big Bend National Park and was granted my wish by David Tinsley who flew me out to Lajitas to photograph the old mission ruins at Ruidosa, Texas. Except for a few changes I made, this scene is just up the river from Lajitas, Texas!

DOLAN FALLS is near the Devil's River State Natural Area which is 22 miles off the pavement, between Del Rio and Sonora, Texas. The Nature Conservancy owns the property and controls access to the Falls. 22,000 gallons of cold water per minute, gush from Dolan Springs, upstream.

LAS CUEVAS EBONY This Texas Ebony Tree is on the banks of the Rio Grande at the town of Los Ebanos and is the anchor for the only hand pulled ferry along the United States border. This river crossing is the spot where General Zachary Taylor invaded Mexico in 1846

RUIDOSA MISSION is in Ruidosa, Texas in the Big Bend Area up river From Presidio. The Texas Historical Commission says that is one of the most significant adobe buildings in the state, as its three arches are likely the widest adobe arches in Texas.

LA LOMITA MISSION is located near Mission, Texas, on the banks of the Rio Grande. Built by traveling priests to stop and rest on their travels up the Rio Grande. This chapel was built in 1899 and is all that remains of a larger complex.

WEST TEXAS

SAWTOOTH MOUNTAIN (elevation 7758 feet) is in the Davis Mountains of west Texas and is one of the most picturesque in the range. I wanted to show the scale of this mountain so I added the cattle and cowboys for comparison.

G BOUTWELL

MISSION SAN ELIZARIO is southeast of El Paso and the current chapel was built in 1877 in what was then Mexico. Due to a shift in the Rio Grande, it is now in Texas! The first Thanksgiving Holiday in the Americas was celebrated here.

SALT FLAT TEXAS is on U.S. 62/180 at the foot of the Guadalupe Mountains, about 100 miles east of El Paso and is in some of the most beautiful and rugged country in Texas. If you pass Salt Flat, you'd better go back, because it's a long way to the next watering hole.

PRIDE OF THE OPEN RANGE Pronghorn Antelopes, America's fastest land animal, were almost extinct but, thanks to conservation efforts have made a strong comeback. This scene is between Van Horn and the Guadalupe Mountains!

PRESIDIO COUNTY COURTHOUSE, of Second Empire Style, is on the square in Marfa, Texas. Designed by Alfred Giles and built in 1886, this Courthouse is at the end of a wide boulevard and is sited much like the State Capitol.

ROAD TO TRANQUILITY I found this majestic Live Oak between Grapetown and Luckenbach and knew, that with a few changes, it would make a good painting. I changed the paved road to a dirt road, raised up the hills, moved in the historic stone house from Grapetown, changed the lighting and added more Bluebonnets. Otherwise, it's exactly like I saw it!

THE POLITICIAN I saw this Grackle by the State Capitol, all dressed in his power suit, puffed up squacking and I immediately thought he was a natural born Politician. He sounds pretty good, but you probably can't belive him and besides, he's sitting on the fence!

HAMILTON POOL is a collapsed cavern and quite an awesome sight! The Waterfall is about 50 feet high and I've only shown about a third of the overhang! This is now a Travis County Park and is west of Austin on Hamilton Pool road

LONG'S FALLS are on the Llano River just upstream from Kingsland, Texas. and are accessible from Long's Fishing Camp. This is just a portion of the falls, as it would be impossible to get them all into one picture. The Llano River is one of the most scenic rivers in Texas!

MISSION SAN JOSE is in San Antonio and was established in 1720. It is the largest of the Texas Missions and is often referred to as "The Queen of Missions" and it is now part of the United States National Parks system.

SCENES FROM OUR HIGHVIEW RANCH

BOSQUE BLANKET
This is a view of our ranch in Bosque County near Clifton, Texas. On a good year, In late May and early June the Indian Blankets bloom and seem to set the landscape on fire with color!

SPRING BREAK
This last spring (1991) I found our ten Longhorns resting beneath our favorite oak grove and this painting is the result. I wouldn't be surprised if cattle inspired the custom of Siesta, because these guys always lay down at mid afternoon for a little nap. I added the little house in the background to give this picture some depth!

BARN CATS On the day Martha and I found our ranch, we first looked at the house and then went down to the barn. I walked inside, turned around, saw this scene and said to Martha, "There's a Painting, just waiting to be painted!"

ETHNIC DIVERSITY These three calves were fathered by a brown Limosin Bull. The black calf had a Black Angus mother, the brown calf had a brown mother, but the white calf's mother was solid brown with a white patch on her forehead. We never figured out how these two brown animals had a solid white calf!

HIGH AND DRY This is our porch and when it rains we can usually count on wild birds seeking refuge, unless our not-so-wild cats get there first, in which case the birds will be found at the tops of the columns!

FOGGY MORNING These are our Longhorn steers drifting up to my truck to be fed one very foggy morning. I knew immediately, that this had to be a Painting!

LONE STAR CLASSIC This scene is from the pasture behind our 1905 ranch house but I added the windmill, which I intend to add for real someday!

CARBON COPY I was feeding my cattle one morning when this cow and her calf caught my eye. Like all babies, the calf was curious about everything and like any good mother, the cow was intent on securing the safety of her baby. As I got a little too close, the cow charged me and I had to duck behind our bull for safety. I was amused by the paradox of the situation, in that I was hiding behind a bull, normally considered to be an aggressive beast, (our bull was as tame and gentle as they come) while being pursued by a cow, normally considered to be a passive creature! When the unexpected happens as surely it will, I have found that it is much easier to deal with, if I can find something about it that is amusing or humorous.

PATH LESS TRAVELLED This century old iron gate, is the gate to our front yard here on the ranch and is seldom used anymore because of the 20 feet of stairs to climb to get to it. These days we all drive up to the back gate, where it is flat and easy to access. These Irises were planted by Mellie Pool over 100 years ago and bless our yard every spring.

THE LUCKY ONE

Our society places so much emphasis on youth
that it's easy to get the impression
that getting old is some kind of disgrace.

This seems strange to me, because
everyone gets to be young
but only the luckiest people, get to be old.

In my opinion each day,
no matter how many problems it may pose,
is truly a blessing,
because no one is promised tomorrow
and to live to be very old
is to have been blessed many times!

May each day be a blessing
and may you live to be very, very old!

-George Boutwell